U:P:D:A:T:E

Urb ... y ... r

Case studies ... et Union

David M. Smith

*The right of the
University of Cambridge
to print and sell
all manner of books
was granted by
Henry VIII in 1534.
The University has printed
and published continuously
since 1584.*

CAMBRIDGE UNIVERSITY PRESS

Cambridge New York Port Chester Melbourne Sydney

Published by the Press Syndicate of the University of Cambridge
The Pitt Building, Trumpington Street, Cambridge   CB2 1RP
40 West 20th Street, New York, NY 10011, USA
10 Stamford Road, Oakleigh, Melbourne 3166, Australia

First published 1989

Printed in Great Britain at the University Press, Cambridge

British Library cataloguing in publication data

Smith, David M. (David Marshall), *1936-*
   Urban inequality under socialism: case studies from Eastern
Europe. -- (Update)
   1. Eastern Europe. Urban regions. Social aspects
I. Title II. Series
   307.7'6'0947

ISBN 0 521 36679 8

Library of Congress catalog card number: 69-15827

ACKNOWLEDGEMENTS

The author is grateful to the many colleagues in Eastern Europe and the Soviet Union whose guided tours, explanations of their research findings and generous hospitality have contributed to his understanding and enjoyment of their cities. Special thanks are due to Natasha Barbash, Leonid Chorniy, Boleslaw Domanski, the late Veniamin Gokhman, Pavel Il'in, Marek Jerczinski, Jacek Malczewski, Iwona Sagan and Gregorz Weclawowicz, and to Andrzej Jagielski and Marat Tajin who provided helpful critiques of the chapters on Poland and the Soviet Union respectively. Responsibility for the interpretations contained in this volume is the author's alone.

NOTE ON NAMES

Russian names of people and places have been transliterated from the Cyrillic alphabet by usual conventions. Those from Czechoslovakia, Hungary and Poland have been 'anglicised' so as to simplify typography; they may be pronounced quite differently from the way they read here.

Cover
'House where A. C. Pushkin lived' (Arbat 53, Moscow) by Evgeniy Kumankov, in memory of Professor Veniamin Maksimovich Gokhman, who introduced the author to many parts of Moscow and to the work of this Soviet artist.

PREFACE

The need to keep up to date with new trends and developments in geography or in aspects of geographical study is a constant problem for the teacher. This is particularly so where access to information on new techniques, ideas or sources of data is difficult and where contact with colleagues in higher education is limited. **Update** aims to improve this contact by providing brief, frequently revised booklets on topics directly linked to the 'A' level syllabus and college courses. They range from the compilation and interpretation of up-to-date statistical information of direct use in the classroom to the discussion of recent research work which may shed new light on the received ideas of the text-book. They are readable and cheap. Topics range over both physical and human geography, though coverage will reflect the specialisms of the staff in the Department of Geography at Queen Mary College where the series is produced.

Urban Inequality under Socialism covers a topic largely neglected in geography text-books. Shortage of readily accessible information as well as the tendency to concentrate on the advanced capitalist or 'western' world means that both school and university exposure to the cities of Eastern Europe and the Soviet Union in geography courses is often very limited. This **Update** provides a series of case studies selected to illustrate and interpret aspects of the spatial form of the East European and Soviet city as it has developed under socialism. The focus on inequality in living standards is chosen so as to confront a central paradox of socialism in practice - the existence of inequality under a system of government supposedly dedicated to egalitarianism. The content combines a review of some of the more important contributions to the literature with the author's own research and first-hand experience.

Roger Lee
Murray Gray

Editors, **Update**

THE AUTHOR

David M. Smith is Professor of Geography at Queen Mary College, University of London. His previous appointments were at the University of Manchester, Southern Illinois University, the University of Florida, the University of Natal, the University of the Witwatersrand and the University of New England. He has undertaken a number of study visits to Eastern Europe, and is especially interested in inequality in Soviet and Polish cities as part of an ongoing international comparative study of the relationship between social structure and spatial form with special reference to the metropolis.

Professor Smith has written or edited numerous books in the fields of economic and social geography. These include **Industrial Location: An Economic Geographical Analysis** (1971, Wiley, 2nd edition 1981), **Human Geography: A Welfare Approach** (1977, Arnold), **Where the Grass is Greener: Living in an Unequal World** (1979, Penguin), and, of special relevance to the present volume, **Geography, Inequality and Society** (1988, Cambridge University Press). His earlier contribution to the **Update** series is **Apartheid in South Africa** (1985, revised 1987).

CONTENTS

1. SOCIALISM AND THE CITY

'to make men Socialists is nothing, but to make Socialism human is a great thing'
Oscar Wilde (1899)

'we have yet to create the socialist city'
B. S. Khorev (1975)

Cities are very much a reflection of the societies that create them. The built form of the environment provides a means of giving conspicuous and (often literally) concrete expression to people's aspirations and values. This is perhaps most obvious at the local scale - in statues of politicians, soldiers and poets or in the monumental architecture of civic buildings and commercial edifices. But in more subtle yet readily discernible ways the broader spatial form or morphology of cities reflects something of the people and purpose behind their construction, and indeed the extent to which this has arisen from some conscious collective action.

The image of the East European city

The popular image of the city in Eastern Europe and the Soviet Union, as viewed from the 'west', tends to be one of drab uniformity. Television, cinema and other visual media reveal landscapes of row upon row of apartment blocks (not unlike the council flats in parts of British cities or public housing in the United States), interrupted only by factories, rather forbidding public buildings, and pictures of Lenin along with slogans exhorting the masses to hard work and new heights of revolutionary zeal. Such images are comfortably consistent with our accepted understanding of the societies concerned - of a colourless and functional uniformity in which human individuality is severely constrained by the political domination of 'the Party' and its apparatus of state control. Yet just as this picture of the socialist city is vastly oversimplified, so is that of socialist society itself. Both are caricatures, which emphasise certain features and hence give them undue prominence, at the expense of detail which is an important part of the truth.

Contrasting symbols of socialism in the urban landscape: **Plate 1** *(left) statue of workers and Communist Party slogan in central square of the city of Kovets in the Ukrainian Soviet Socialist Republic of the USSR;* **Plate 2** *(right) memorial to workers killed in an uprising at the Lenin Shipyard in Gdansk, birthplace of the trade union Solidarity which poses a challenge to the Party in Poland.*

Of course, societies characterised by central planning in pursuit of egalitarian objectives might be expected to reveal spatial order tending towards uniformity. But planning, and planners, are seldom if ever so powerful, purposeful or consistent, nor the populace at large so compliant. Human individuality and creativity as well as fallibility find expression even in the most rigidly planned or controlled societies, giving variety to what might otherwise be a largely undifferentiated urban landscape. The evidence of this, in the detailed layout and texture of a city, provides an important reading on how the society actually functions - on how closely lived experience conforms to what the prevailing ideology prescribes.

The focus on inequality

To focus attention on inequality in this volume allows us to confront what is perhaps the central paradox or contradiction of socialist society: the continuing existence of inequality in living standards under a system dedicated in principle to egalitarian objectives. Such a perspective gives our analysis a special cutting edge. It takes us to the heart of the relationship between social structure and spatial form, or the nature of a society and its geography. In the process, we will learn enough of the East European city in its broader aspects to make informed comparisons with those familiar to us from our own experience as well as from their predominance in the text-books. And we will learn more of socialist society this way than if we concentrated on traditional aspects of urban morphology and development.

But, just what do we mean by inequality? Geographers are accustomed to dealing with differences; the subject of geography is itself often defined as the study of areal differentiation. However, to say that areas, or the people living in them, are *different* is not necessarily to say that they are *unequal*. People may engage in different economic activities and have different ways of life, but we do not usually describe these in terms of inequality. It is when we consider living standards, measured by such criteria as income, health, housing, education or material posessions, that the issue of inequality arises. In other words, inequality refers to the availability or consumption of things to which we assign value, such that the more (or less) people get, the better (or worse) off they are. People who freely spend their money on different leisure pursuits, for example, would be regarded as different, but not unequal unless some had more leisure than others who valued it just the same, or more money to spend on it. People may also differ, in the sense of being unequal, with respect to such attributes as social status and economic or political power, which may have a bearing on their living standards, as well as with respect to more abstract qualities such as freedom and human rights. Further discussion of the meaning of inequality, its measurement and its social significance can be found in Smith (1988, pp. 8-25).

In the case studies presented in subsequent chapters, the emphasis will be on variations from place to place in aspects of consumption, the nature of which justifies the interpretation of inequality. Particular attention will be placed on housing, the means whereby unequal access to housing of varying quality arises and the consequent patterns of segregation in urban residential space. Housing is important not only to living standards but also provides conspicuous visual evidence of inequality in cities where the first impression of uniformity may be deceptive. Evidence on other conditions such as availability of services, environmental quality and occupational status, will be provided where possible, but limits to the data available constantly constrain what can be said with any precision about inequality in the socialist city.

The meaning of socialism

Before proceeding further, however, it is necessary to say something about what we mean by socialism. Socialism is not to be confused with communism, which is an 'ideal' form of society originally envisaged by Karl Marx as the ultimate outcome of the demise of capitalism and supposed to be classless, with common ownership of property and without the necessity for state government. Nor should socialism be confused with the activities of some 'left-wing' councils in Britain, for example, acting out 'radical' policies with respect to such matters as social service provision within the constraints of a capitalist society. The meaning of socialism adopted here may initially be defined as a social-economic-political system in which the capacity to produce and deliver goods and services is substantially within state ownership and control. The state will own the land and other natural resources, the basic industries, and the means of producing most consumer goods and virtually all services, with output and prices centrally determined. However, there will be some private enterprise (especially in agriculture), and private ownership of personal property may extend to housing. The central motive force of such societies is supposed to be collective action for the general good, rather than the individualistic pursuit of private gain which characterises capitalism.

Socialism in the sense identified here is sometimes portrayed as an intermediate or transitional stage between capitalism and 'true' communism. The main difference between this kind of society and communism is that in the latter people should contribute according to their ability and receive goods and services according to their need (to paraphrase Marx), whereas under socialism people are rewarded for their labour in relation to the quantity and quality of the work they perform. Thus if people contribute unequally they will be treated unequally, at least with respect to earnings and probably in other aspects of life. Nevertheless, equality is an important element in the ideology or political rhetoric of socialist societies. And they are generally run by a Communist Party, dedicated in principle, if not necessarily in practice, to completing the transformation to full communism.

There is much more to socialism than this, of course, as will be revealed later in this and subsequent chapters. But the above is sufficient to enable us to begin to consider whether there is likely to be something fundamentally different about cities in the socialist countries of Eastern Europe and the Soviet Union.

The 'socialist city'

The question of whether there is a distinctive 'socialist city' was first drawn prominently to the attention of geographers by French and Hamilton (1979), in a book which still provides an authoritative and informative review. They drew attention to the neglect of the cities of the socialist world, compared with the voluminous literature on towns and urban structure not only in North America and Western Europe, but also in the developing world. The reasons for this neglect include language constraints on reading original source material, problems of data shortage, the relative inaccessibility of some of the countries concerned, and the difficulty which western scholars and teachers often have in dealing with socialism dispassionately and objectively if at all. More recently the literature on urbanisation, planning and housing in Eastern Europe has grown, but as French (1987, p. 310) has pointed out, the internal geography of the city has still received only restricted attention.

The cities of Eastern Europe and the Soviet Union are, therefore, almost a contemporary *terra incognita*, with the prospect of discovering something new and exciting. The basic features of socialism outlined above certainly give rise to the expectation of a distinctive kind of city, the more so if we add a little detail. Urban living has a particular significance in Marxist/socialist ideology. It is seen as a progressive force encouraging collective rather than individual identity, and city planning is an important means of achieving this political purpose. Central planning along with state ownership of land means that urbanisation can be subjected to a greater degree of control than under capitalism. Urban growth and reconstruction have proceeded rapidly in most socialist countries as part of a programme of industrialisation. Each city has its place in a planned urban hierarchy connected with a process of regional development planning which is supposed to narrow the difference in living standards between town and countryside.

The internal structure of the socialist city will be planned to facilitate the delivery of social services as well as to ensure the efficient operation of the economy. Public transport is more important than in the capitalist city as a way of ensuring ready access to work, leisure and other sources of the satisfaction of human needs. The public provision of housing is one of the most important means whereby the state seeks to ensure satisfactory living standards for all, and this gives a special character to the residential areas.

A picture of how the ideal socialist city might be organised is provided by Demko and Regulska (1987, p. 290):

The abolition of private property, removal of privileged classes, and application of equity principles espoused by Marxist/socialist leaders should radically alter urban patterns. In the housing arena, the expectation would be one of non-discriminatory, non-spatially differentiated housing in general. No social or occupational group would have better or more favorably located residential sites so that one would find a randomly distributed housing pattern. Similarly, public services of all kinds, including transportation, should be of equal quality, availability and accessibility. Commuting to work ... would be minimized and no group would be more dependent on or penalized by such travel than others. Such amenities as a high quality physical environment, including recreational environment, would be equally accessible to all. All such urban conditions would be similarly equitably arranged and available.

However, they point out that, given the severe consraints imposed by the physical inheritance from an earlier era, the achievement of such an ideal would require a period of transition.

Of all the reasons why reality might depart from such an ideal, history is probably the most important. Just like Rome, socialism could not be built in a day and nor could its cities. In one of the first text-books to give serious treatment to the socialist city, Rugg (1972, pp. 252-6) makes a basic distinction between 'partially-changed cities' and 'new cities'. Those which have been partially changed by socialism originated in an earlier era, like the long-established capital cities of Moscow, Prague and Warsaw on which there are case studies in this volume. But even within this group there will be differences in the extent to which socialist planning has replaced the pre-existing urban fabric, depending on the extent of war damage and the resources devoted to reconstruction, for example. The new cities have usually been created under socialism for some specific function, such as Akademgorodok, the academic town in Siberia, or Nowa Huta the industrial satellite of Cracow, both of which we will encounter in subsequent chapters. Another contribution of the historical dimension is the time taken to construct the socialist city, or to impose it on the past, with different periods, planning styles and building standards generating different landscapes.

There is a view that the cities of Eastern Europe and the Soviet Union are not fundamentally different from those of the advanced capitalist world, especially Western Europe. They share much of the same historical and physical legacy, and are subject to the same pressures of modern industrial society. Friedrichs (1988, p. 128), for example, claims that:

Except for a short period in the early 1920s ... there are no specific socialist types of land use, distribution of new housing, internal organization of residential blocks, or location of companies. Even the principal goal of socialist city planning - to locate new residential areas close to working areas - has been pursued in Western planning too.

While it may be hard to find evidence of such a highly distinctive urban and residential form as neighbourhoods or blocks of flats built for communal living, to argue that modern industrial cities are all very much the same is to overlook some special features of those in socialist countries, not least with respect to their patterns of inequality.

Towards a model of the socialist city

In attempting to identify and understand the socialist city, an inevitable point of reference will be those cities most familiar to us in our own society. We are accustomed to the patterns of differentiation in cities of the advanced capitalist world summarised in the text-books as concentric zones associated with Burgess and the 'Chicago school' of urban social ecology, or the wedges identified by Hoyt, and with multiple nuclei to complicate the form of the larger metropolis. Social status and living standards vary in a fairly predictable manner, with the poor generally concentrated within or around the inner city, the better off in the suburbs, and the rich in the 'stockbroker belt' beyond or in smart enclaves in the city. Wedges are formed as people with higher incomes occupy and move out to the more attractive areas, leaving others to take the less salubrious sites. We are also aware that stage in life cycle (including age of population and family size) and race or ethnicity find spatial expression in the capitalist city. For the most part, the patterns are an outcome of the fact that land is allocated by market mechanisms to the highest bidder, although some residential sorting and segregation reflect social custom and culture as well as economics.

Can we say enough about the socialist city at the outset, by way of generalisation, to detect any resemblance to the spatial structure of the capitalist city? A useful model of the growth of an East European city has been devised by Hamilton and is illustrated in Figure 1.1. The city comprises several distinctive zones, which he summarises as follows (French and Hamilton, 1979, p. 227):

(1) the historic medieval or renaissance core; (2) inner commercial, housing, and industrial areas from the capitalist period; (3) a zone of socialist transition or renewal, where modern construction is partially and progressively replacing inherited urban or relict-village features; (4) socialist housing of the 1950s; (5) integrated socialist neighbourhoods and residential districts of the 1960s and 1970s [and 1980s]; (6) open or planted 'isolation belts'; (7) industrial or related zones; and (8) open countryside, forest, or hills, including tourist complexes. Broadly speaking, outward expansion of city areas yields a concentric-zonal pattern, successive stages of building being readily recognizable in architectural styles and skylines. This pattern tends to 'overlay' a more sectoral or 'wedge-like' distribution of functional zones associated with particular site qualities, historic traditions, and major transport arteries. Fundamentally distinct, however, are the pre-socialist inner and socialist outer urban areas.

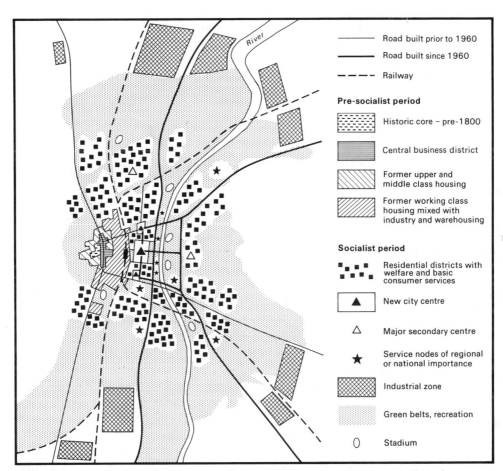

Figure 1.1 A model of the growth of an East European socialist city
Source: French and Hamilton (1979, p. 228, Fig. 9.3)

The inherited inner area will be subject to more differentiation than the socialist outer urban area with its planned uniformity. The historic core and its preservation may have necessitated construction of a new city centre.

Hamilton's model indicates some similarity with the advanced capitalist city, at least to the extent of finding sectors and wedges in the pattern of land use differentiation. But how far is this pattern indicative of inequalities in living standards, of the kind which we have come to associate with the spatial form of the capitalist city? This is a question to be addressed in the remainder of this volume, in which case studies from a number of East European countries have been assembled to attempt to elucidate something of both patterns of inequality and the processes behind them.

Background to the case studies

Eastern Europe is usually defined as the countries of Albania, Bulgaria, Czechoslovakia, the German Democratic Republic (GDR, i.e. East Germany), Hungary, Poland, Romania and Yugoslavia, to which is often added the western parts of the Union of Soviet Socialist Republics (USSR or Soviet Union). For the purpose of this publication, the scope is extended to incorporate any Soviet city. Table 1.1 shows the population of the countries concerned, along with their levels of urbanisation and the populations of their two largest cities. Figure 1.2 provides a basic location map.

Table 1.1   Population, urbanisation and major cities in Eastern Europe and the Soviet Union c.1985

Country	Total popn (m)	Urban popn (%) 1970	Urban popn (%) c.1985	Population of largest cities ('000s) 1st (capital)		2nd city	
Albania	3.0	33.8	34.4	Tirana	216	Durres	75
Bulgaria	9.0	52.3	65.2	Sofia	1115	Plovdiv	342
Czechoslovakia	15.4	55.5	74.1	Prague	1191	Bratislava	413
GDR	16.6	73.6	76.6	Berlin	1223	Leipzig	552
Hungary	10.6	46.9	58.3	Budapest	2074	Miskolc	211
Poland	37.2	52.3	60.1	Warsaw	1650	Lodz	849
Romania	22.6	40.8	49.2	Bucharest	1961	Brasov	335
Yugoslavia	22.4	38.6	46.1	Belgrade	1088	Zagreb	650
USSR	277.5	56.3	65.4	Moscow	8642	Leningrad	4867

Source: **United Nations Demographic Yearbook**, 1973, 1986. Figures for c.1985 refer to the latest available, which is 1985 or 1986 except for a few cases of slightly earlier dates.

Most of the countries in question have experienced substantial increases in the proportion of their population living in urban areas in recent years. This is because it has been during the socialist period that they have undergone the rapid industrialisation, and associated population migration from the countryside, which took place somewhat earlier in much of Western Europe. Under socialism, urbanisation has been very much a planned and directed process, closely related to the transformation and modernisation of societies with large agrarian economies into advanced industrial nations. Another important feature which distinguishes urbanisation here from Western Europe is the rapid growth of certain cities, usually associated with new economic or administrative roles: in the Soviet Union, for example, there are a number of cities with over a million population today which had only a few hundreds of thousands in the 1930s.

The largest city in each country, invariably the capital, often accounts for a relatively high proportion of the total national population and can be many times larger than the second city, as Table 1.2 shows. All the countries concerned have policies of restraining the growth of the capital, as part of a strategy of decentralising economic activity and reducing regional disparities in living standards. However, the importance attached to this policy varies from country to country, as does the extent of domination of the capital and the general level of urbanisation.

Table 1.2 provides comparative information on four of the capital cities featured in case studies. Absolute population growth over the past quarter of a century varies from 2.4 million in Moscow to less than 60,000 in Prague. The largest growth in relative terms has been in Warsaw, which was so severely damaged in the Second World War that its pre-war population had not been restored by 1960. Most of the population growth in Moscow and Warsaw is accounted for by inward migration, which has been very low in Budapest and Prague - reflecting the relative strength or effectiveness of decentralisation policy. There are considerable variations in housing space per resident, with Muscovites worst provided for but having experienced the greatest relative improvement in terms of persons per dwelling.

Figure 1.2 Major cities of Eastern Europe

Table 1.2 Comparative information on four capital cities

	Budapest	*Moscow*	*Prague*	*Warsaw*
Population ('000s):				
1960	1805	6242	1133	1139
1970	1945	7077	1141	1315
1980	2059	8099	1182	1596
1985	2074	8642	1191	1650
Population change:				
1960-1985 ('000s)	269	2400	58	511
1960-1985 (%)	14.9	38.4	5.1	44.9
1982 net in-migration	10947	86130	6921	13840
Dwellings:				
number 1980 ('000s)	727	2542	448	514
persons/dwelling 1960	3.4	7.0	3.4	3.7
persons/dwelling 1980	2.8	3.2	2.6	2.9
square metres/person 1980	19.0	10.0	14.0	15.2

Sources: Friedrichs (1988, pp. 132, 135, Tables 5.3, 5.4, 5.5); 1985 populations from **United Nations Demographic Yearbook**, 1987.

The choice of cases to be considered in the chapters which follow has been highly selective. It is considered better to go into detail in a small number of cases than to provide a comprehensive but much more superficial review. Attention has therefore been confined to the four countries of Czechoslovakia, Hungary, Poland and the Soviet Union, in particular to the last two, and within them to relatively few individual cities. This choice reflects the available literature as well as the intrinsic interest of the cases described.

The rationale behind the sequence of material may be outlined briefly. First, Moscow is taken as somewhat of a showpiece of the socialist city, to see how equality is planned for and to provide an initial indication of some of the reasons why it is not achieved (Chapter 2). In Chapter 3 further evidence of spatial inequality and residential segregation is provided from other selected Soviet cities. Then Chapter 4 takes the case of Prague to illustrate the impact of socialism on an urban form largely inherited from an earlier era. Chapter 5 moves to Hungary to focus on the crucial question of how unequal access to housing of variable quality is a feature of the socialist city. Chapter 6 takes Warsaw to illustrate various aspects of spatial disparities in a city which has been almost entirely rebuilt during the socialist period. Findings from some other Polish cities are reviewed in Chapter 7. Chapter 8 sums up the accumulated evidence and identifies the main features of the processes behind inequality in the socialist city.

Specific issues

Before getting down to detail, it may be helpful to list the specific issues to be raised and illustrated by the case material. These are posed as a series of questions which may act as a study guide:

How does socialist planning seek to achieve equality in living standards within cities?

How does some degree of inequality arise from the planning practice itself and as an inevitable outcome of geography and history?

How does the pre-socialist spatial structure of the city affect the form of the socialist city and its pattern of inequality?

To what extent does urban infrastructure, service provision and general environmental quality vary within the kind of cities under review?

How do people appraise the variable quality of the urban environment, and how do they exercise whatever freedom they have to make residential choices?

What evidence is there to reveal intra-urban patterns of inequality in living standards?

How do different population groups come to occupy different parts of the city, with variable housing and environmental quality?

Is there a discernible pattern of social, occupational or ethnic segregation in residential space?

What can we say about the nature of socialism in practice, on the basis of patterns of inequality in cities?

Some final words of warning are offered, to complete this introduction. The world we are about to enter tends to be clouded by both ignorance and prejudice in the 'west', and such attitudes can impede understanding. It will therefore assist if the material which follows is read with as open a mind as possible. In particular, predispositions to viewing Eastern Europe and the Soviet Union as some monolithic bloc deprived of variety and humanity should fade before the actual experience which we open up. We shall learn that there are differences in the national experience of socialism which have a bearing on the development of the city. But, above all, we will see how the drawing-board ideals have yielded, to a greater or lesser extent, to the actions of the people themselves as they seek individual, family or group advantage within what flexibility and freedom of choice the system permits. If the socialist city has not yet been created as an ideal, the reality which we observe shows that socialism is indeed being made human.

2. MOSCOW: SHOWPIECE OF SOVIET SOCIALISM

Moscow is the obvious starting point for any discussion of inequality in the socialist city. As capital of the USSR, and of the largest and most populous of its fourteen constituent republics (the RSFSR or Russian Republic), Moscow is very much a show-place of Soviet socialism. This is true not only in the sense that the Soviet authorities have used Moscow to demonstrate what they consider to be the best of socialist urban planning, but also because it reveals with particular effect the kind of place the socialist city elsewhere may become. We will move straight into this case, leaving a general introduction to urbanisation in the Soviet Union for the beginning of the next chapter.

Background

On the eve of the Revolution in 1917 Moscow was one of the largest cities in Europe, with a population of about 1.6 million. By 1939 it had reached 4.5 million and this has subsequently doubled. If the built-up area beyond the official city limits is included, the population is now (1989) well over 13 million, and this is expected to reach 15 or 16 million by the end of the century despite the long-standing policy of restricting the growth of the capital. Most of the recent and projected future growth is accounted for by migration, for Moscow shares with large cities in many parts of the world a magnetic attraction to people from smaller towns and the countryside seeking a better life.

Something of the scale of the recent growth of Moscow is indicated in Table 2.1. Each column refers to a five-year planning period. In the quarter of a century since the beginning of the 1960s the population of the city has grown by more than 2.5 million. Over 2.4 million new flats have been constructed, with a steadily increasing average size, enabling no less than 7.5 million people to move to new and presumably improved accommodation.

Table 2.1 **Population growth and new housing in Moscow 1961-1985**

	1961-65	1966-70	1971-75	1976-80	1981-85
Population increase	540000	595000	557600	472500	400500
New flats built	560000	571000	538000	404000	308000
Average size (m^2)	44.6	45.4	48.2	52.5	56.0
People moving to new flats ('000s)	2000	1790	1620	1119	920

Source: Thomas (1988, p. 221, Table 1)

Present-day Moscow is very much a product of the socialist or 'Soviet' period. Figure 2.1 shows the limited extent of the pre-Revolutionary city, and much of what was inherited from Tsarist times has subsequently been rebuilt. For many years the ring road marked the official boundary of the city, and this was supposed to be the outer limit to urban development but in 1984 some extension took place in recognition of the reality of continuing growth. The map indicates something of the scale of the series of satellite towns which now virtually surround the city. For further background on development and planning in Moscow, reference can be made to Hall (1984), Thomas (1988) and to Hamilton (1976) which still provides the only substantial general geographical account of the city-region readily accessible in English other than somewhat unrevealing Soviet publications. While the full implications of the present era of national restructuring (*perestroika*) for the city are as yet unclear, some indications are provided by Bond (1988).

To address the question of inequality in living standards within the city of Moscow requires reference to a limited and scattered literature, most of it the outcome of discrete Soviet research (not all of which is available in English translation or even summary). Selectivity has been exercised, and generalisation is inevitable, not only because of the sheer scale of the city but also because of the shortage of 'hard' data. Published information has been supplemented by first-hand field investigations and by anecdotal evidence. Earlier versions of some of what follows may be found in Smith (1979 and 1988).

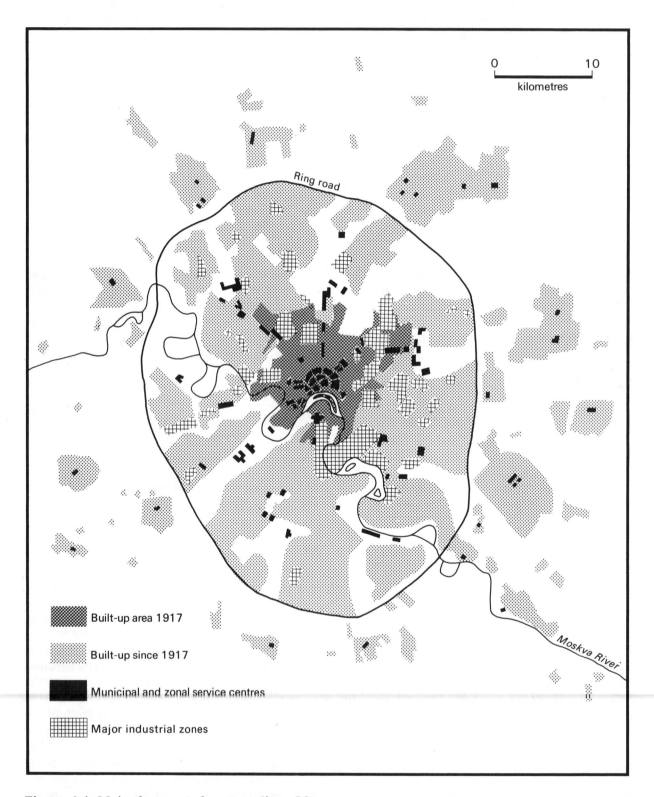

Figure 2.1 Main features of metropolitan Moscow
Source: various Soviet publications

Planning for equality

Following the Revolution in 1917, the first practical step towards a more equal society was the confiscation and reallocation of large houses of wealthy families in inner parts of the city, which were reoccupied by poorer people particularly from the outer suburbs. The need for comprehensive urban planning was quickly recognised and to facilitate this, land was nationalised and much of the economy and infrastructure was also taken over by the state or municipal authorities. However, industrialisation had immediate priority, and it was 1935 before a general plan was approved for Moscow and well after the Second World War before substantial impact was made on the city's enormous and long-standing housing problem.

It was Khrushchev who initiated the major programme of post-war housing development in the late 1950s. The scale of construction indicated in Table 2.1 above has transformed the landscape of the city, as substandard low-rise accommodation in the inner areas has been demolished and the people rehoused in successively taller blocks of flats. The layout of the service infrastructure, including the transportation system, has been designed to facilitate easy access from residence to workplace and to the various facilities providing for people's needs. There is a flexible (if often overcrowded) network of conventional and trolley 'buses supplementing the Metro for the equivalent of a few pence a journey anywhere in the city.

Plate 3 (l) Typical microraion, *basic element of Soviet urban planning, in the Tronaryovo district of Moscow's south-western suburbs, with school, playing fields and other facilities within easy reach of residents of the housing blocks.* **Plate 4** *(r) Transportation is important to Muscovites in getting to work and to non-local services: here is a busy link between the 'bus service and the Metro where a line to the southern suburbs terminates.*

The basic building block of the Soviet city is the *microraion* (microregion or district). After some early experiments with communal living, which was thought to be an effective means of getting people to behave collectively, the *microraion* became a major planning device in the 1950s, and has remained so with some modifications ever since. It comprises a neighbourhood unit of living space in the form of blocks of flats, along with associated services, for a population of perhaps 5000 to 15,000. They are essentially pedestrian precincts, containing restaurants, nurseries, kindergartens, club rooms, libraries and sports facilities, as well as educational, health, retail and cultural services. The level of provision is usually on a per capita basis involving specific 'norms' for the number of restaurant seats, square metres of shopping space and health service personnel, for example. Thus people should all have a wide range of day-to-day needs satisfied within their immediate locality, often within a short walk of where they live. This, together with per capita norms for living space within similar or identical blocks of flats, suggests something approaching equality in living standards as the likely and, of course, desired outcome.

The actual layout, design and scale of the *microraion* varies with period of construction, but those illustrated in Figure 2.2 are representative.

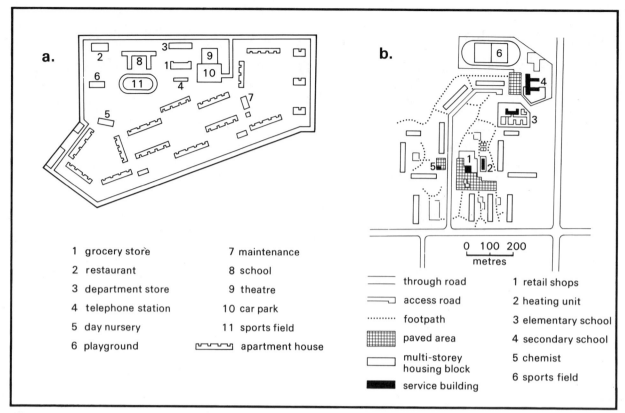

Figure 2.2 Examples of *microraion* planning, a. in the 1950s, b. in the late 1960s
Sources: a. Rugg (1972, p. 251, Fig. 6.10), b. Hamilton (1978, p. 515)

At a broader spatial scale, each *microraion* forms part of a nested hierarchy or layered system of service provision. As in the capitalist city, every facility cannot be provided locally for it is more efficient to locate specialised and less frequently used services selectively in relation to larger populations. Thus several micro-districts may be aggregated to form a larger residential complex or district of perhaps 30,000 to 50,000 population, for the provision of a wider range of services within a radius of 1000 to 1200 metres compared with 150 to 200 metres for the *microraion* (French and Hamilton, 1979, pp. 60-1). One variant of this type of hierarchical structure is illustrated in Bater (1980, p. 102). Residential districts are aggregated up into urban districts of 100,000 to 300,000 inhabitants, which themselves form part of urban zones with perhaps a million people in a major sector of the city. In health care, for example, the 'polyclinic' providing basic outpatient services may cater for the 20,000 to 50,000 population of three micro-districts, with general hospitals serving a wider area of perhaps 300,000 and major specialist hospitals in each of the larger zones.

Sources of inequality in service provision

While the individual *microraion* can reasonably be expected to deliver something like equal access to the elements of urban infrastructure built into it, this is not the case with respect to the broader hierarchy of service provision. Here there is a contradiction between the need to locate certain facilities centrally in relation to relatively large populations in the interests of efficiency, and the more even distribution (at the higher cost implicit in the loss of economies of scale) required to approach equal access. At the extreme, it is hard to envisage more than one Bolshoi Theatre or Lenin Library even in a city as large as Moscow, and some people will be closer to these facilities than will others. Thus the ideal of equality begins to founder on the reality of the necessarily uneven distribution of at least some services.

Another source of inequality in the planned spatial distribution of services is the time lag between construction of the housing blocks and the related services. This arises from failure to coordinate different elements in the construction process, as well as from the priority traditionally afforded to housing in the Soviet Union. Newer residential areas around the city fringe are commonly disadvantaged in this way, as part of the widely recognised general problem of under-provision of norms. There is also the fact that quality of services can vary among districts, and that facilities provided locally for workers at a particular factory, for example, will not be open to other people living nearby. A further source of differential access to services arises from the random or fortuitous appearance of such facilities as unofficial markets for anything from pets to scarce (or banned) books, as people find their own ways of matching demand and supply in an economy not well tuned to consumer preferences.

From the above it might reasonably be concluded that people in some parts of Moscow will have better access to services than others elsewhere. In particular the inner parts of the city should be at an advantage, for it is here that the more specialised facilities will tend to be concentrated in a hierarchical structure, and from here that accessibility to other parts of the city will be best because of the focus of transportation lines. What evidence is there to support this expectation?

Figure 2.3 offers two indications of the form of areal differentiation in service provision within the city of Moscow (as bounded by the ring road). Figure 2.3a shows the regions or boroughs into which the city is divided for administrative purposes, shaded according to an *index of urban infrastructure* reflecting density of public transport lines and Metro stations and such facilities as laundries, shops, cafes, kindergartens, libraries and cinemas. The distinction between inner and outer parts of the city is clear, the latter having generally lower levels of provision than the former. A more detailed picture at a finer spatial scale is provided in Figure 2.3b, which shows an index of what the Soviet scholars responsible describe as *urban character*. This combines information on 'the degree of physical development of the urban environment and the duration of its evolution'; tracts with high values are 'distinguished by the presence of theatres, a built-up area in keeping with Moscow's prominence as the nation's capital, a well-rounded urban environment and a high density of retail outlets selling manufactured goods' (Barbash and Gutnov, 1980, pp. 567-8). Such tracts are concentrated in the central part of the city, with outliers in places where major transport nodes ensure good access. In judging central services, however, it must be recognised that they are heavily used by commuters and visitors from outside the city, as well as by local residents.

Inequalities in housing

If access to the general service infrastructure of the city is differentiated, and unequal, how about housing? Living space is allocated according to a per capita entitlement, the minimum amount

Unequal access to health services in the Soviet city: **Plate 5** *(l) polyclinic providing primary care for local residents in a south-western suburb of Moscow;* **Plate 6** *(r) the so-called 'Kremlin Clinic' in central Moscow, providing what is reputed to be a superior service for members of the political elite.*

having been set at 9 square metres in 1922. While this had been achieved as an average standard in Moscow by 1970, there is evidence of large numbers of families falling well below (with others consequently above the average), so that 'within Moscow there are still very large differences in housing space on a per capita basis' (Bater, 1986, p. 96).

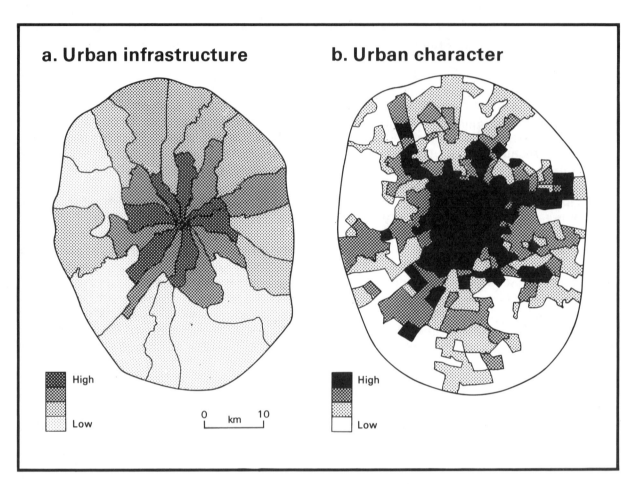

Figure 2.3 Level of development of urban infrastructure and service provision in Moscow
Source: Smith (1988, p. 78, Fig. 5.3), after N.B. Barbash

*The poorest accommodation in the Soviet city: **Plate 7** (l) rural-type housing with garden plots on the edge of Novosibirsk; **Plate 8** (r) pre-Revolutionary house divided into flats (see separate entrances) in one of the remaining old quarters of Moscow.*

Inequality in living space is exacerbated by variations in quality of accommodation. As rent is so low as to account for less than 5 percent of a normal family income, any differences in quality or in locational attributes will arguably be more significant than under a market system in which people's housing tends to vary with what they pay for it. Housing quality in Moscow (and elsewhere in the USSR and other East European countries) varies on the two main dimensions of type of tenure and period of construction.

Housing tenure in the USSR divides roughly into three-quarters 'socialised' and one-quarter privately owner-occupied. Private housing is often of timber construction and of poor quality by conventional (state) standards. It is now confined largely to the fringes of cities, to small towns and to the countryside; very little survives in Moscow. The socialised housing sector can be divided into three parts: government, industrial and cooperative. About 60 percent of Moscow housing is owned by the city government, including most of that associated with *microraion* planning, and about a quarter by industrial and other ministries which have built for their own workers. While industrial and other enterprises may have an incentive to provide good-quality housing (and often services such as health care at the place of work) so as to recruit and maintain an effective labour force, such conditions could be offset by high levels of pollution and other environmental disadvantages of housing often built in close proximity to factories. But period of construction seems more likely to be a source of differentiation in housing stock than the institution responsible for it.

While in general the later the construction the better the quality of housing, this is not always the case. For example in the 1930s under Stalin a number of large apartment blocks were built in ornate style and to relatively high standards, for members of the Party and other privileged groups. Those constructed during the early period of large-scale residential development initiated by Khrushchev are often much less desirable. They are characteristically of five storeys with no lifts, and were rapidly built and shoddily finished; they are now deteriorating and in need of replacement, and widely regarded as slums (French, 1987, p. 312). More recently constructed accommodation in micro-districts on the edge of the city is generally taller and more attractive. It compares very favourably in appearance with modern council estates in Britain, the more so with American 'public housing', although the individual flats are smaller.

The third element of socialised housing, the co-operative, is the main source of qualitative differentiation. Co-operative housing is constructed on behalf of groups of individuals, usually based on the association of workplace (e.g. a particular enterprise or ministry) who thereby acquire collective ownership of their complex or block. Membership requires an initial monetary deposit, which can be considerable, and monthly payments about two-and-a-half times that for a state apartment. Co-operative housing is concentrated in the largest Soviet cities; it accounts for over 8 percent of all housing in Moscow, or a population of about 700,000. While it tends not to be conspicuously different from the best state housing in external appearance, co-operative housing is usually built to higher standards. The deposit for a co-operative is often paid by parents to enable a newly-married son or daughter to avoid the wait for state housing and at the same time get something better. This type of tenure is thus an important and growing source of social inequality.

Environmental differentiation and appraisal

Before considering the question of social stratification in space more generally, it is worth asking how Muscovites themselves appraise the variable environment of housing and associated locational attributes such as service provision. Direct survey evidence on space preference is not available, but there are interesting indications in some Soviet research. The most recent such study is by Vasil'yev and Privalova (1984) who were concerned with the extent to which the locally variable volume and structure of goods and services available satisfies people's needs, and with how this relates to their evaluation of different parts of the city. The spatial scale of analysis is the city borough, and the first step was to group these on the basis of similarities. From data on various criteria significant for the quality of life of city residents, five general factors of territorial differentiation were derived, as follows:

1. *Proximity to elements of the functional-spatial frame*, i.e. the network of major thoroughfares

and transport nodes connecting with shops, service establishments and cultural facilities of citywide or borough rank. As might be expected the central boroughs have the highest levels on this factor.

2. *Development of the urban fabric*, including type of built-up area, i.e. characteristics of buildings, streets, neighbourhoods and the distribution of service establishments and shops of local significance. The pattern is similar to that of factor 1, but to a large extent reflects the time when the area was built up rather than position in relation to the functional organisation of the city.

3. *Saturation with places of employment*, i.e. concentration of economic activity, which is particularly pronounced in the eastern and south-eastern boroughs as well as in the central part of the city.

4. *Transport connections of the territory*, i.e. the relationship between high speed (mainly Metro) and ordinary (trolley or 'bus) means of transport and the convenience of the links between them, which is particularly important to the long-distance commuter. The northern and southern segments of the peripheral boroughs are most poorly served in this respect.

5. *Ecological situation*, including climate and such physical conditions as the presence of large industrial areas or forests.

Figure 2.4 groups boroughs on these factors. Table 2.2 shows how each group performs on a 'factor-combination code' in which groups are rated simply as 'better' (1) or 'worse' (0) on each factor. Thus the central group (I) rates well (or better) on all but the environment factor. Group II on the eastern fringe of the central area is similar to group I except that it is worse with respect to proximity to the city's functional frame. Moving down the table, groups have successively more 0 ratings, until group VII, comprising the northern and southern peripheral boroughs, does worst on all five factors.

Table 2.2   Social valuation of the territory of the city of Moscow

Borough group	Factor -combination code					Number of preferences per 1,000 families	Social valuation
	1	*2*	*3*	*4*	*5*		
I	1	1	1	1	0	6.18	
II	0	1	1	1	0	5.00	0.56
III	0	0	1	1	1	6.89	0.38
IV	0	1	0	1	0	5.25	0.38
V	0	0	0	1	0	3.87	-0.48
VI	0	0	0	0	0	4.53	-0.54
VII	0	0	0	0	0	1.98	-0.57

Source: Vasil'yev and Privalova (1984, p. 493)

This pattern of differentiation was related to people's preferences by considering evidence provided by declarations of intent to exchange accommodation. While government flats are allocated without much regard for where people would like to live, there is a mechanism for exchange. The authors examined more than 15,000 applications in the Moscow City Bureau for Apartment Exchanges, and calculated an indicator of preference based on the difference between the number of people recording a wish to move into a borough group and the number wishing to move out (in September 1980). Expressing this as a ratio per 1000 families gives an indication of relative preferences for each group of boroughs (Table 2.2). The results are broadly consistent with the ratings of the territories on the various factors.

Finally, an attempt was made to isolate a more objective 'social valuation', by examining the advantages of boroughs. The method is complicated and will not be explained here; the outcome is

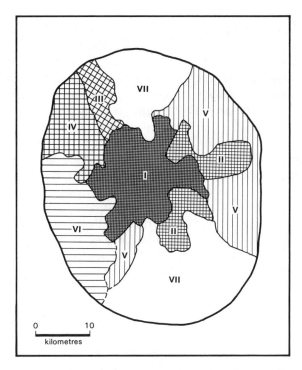

Figure 2.4 Grouping of Moscow city boroughs by combination of preference factors (identified in Table 2.2)
Source: Vasil'yev and Privalova (1984, p. 492, Fig. 1)

a measure of the extent to which residents are likely to have their needs satisfied, given the availability of goods, services and so on. The result is shown in the final column of Table 2.2. As might be expected, it reflects fairly closely the performance of groups on the factor-combination code. The most conspicuous differences with the preference indicator are for groups II and VI: it appears that Muscovites express a preference for the group II boroughs somewhat less than might be expected from the conditions there, while the reverse is the case for group VI.

Vasil'yev and Privalova (1984, p. 495) sum up their findings as follows:

> Muscovites appear to show the greatest preference for the central boroughs in view of the presence of four of the basic factors (except for the ecological situation). Even though each of these factors also has a negative component (for example, the factor of proximity to elements of the urban frame also reflects such phenomena as noise, crowding on streets, in the means of transport, etc.), the availability of all these factors turns out to be attractive and accounts for the high valuation of the central boroughs. These boroughs fall into two groups, with the western group (I), endowed with a more highly developed social infrastructure and somewhat lower employment opportunities, receiving the highest score. ... The lowest valuation was given to the southern and northern boroughs of the outer ring in which residents feel shortage of virtually all the goods included in the model.

Moscow boroughs are quite large, of awkward shape, and subject to internal variations. An analysis of announcements of wishes to move into areas at a finer spatial scale has been undertaken by N. B. Barbash, indicating the highest preferences for selected peripheral wedges rather than for the central parts of the city (see Smith, 1988, p. 83, Fig. 5.4). She attributes this to such environmental disadvantages as noise, pollution and lack of greenery in the centre. An earlier study by Barbash at the borough level showed a close correspondence between the pattern of people wishing to move in and of those wishing to move out (see Smith, 1979, p. 238, Fig. 4.15). This suggests that different groups of people appraise the urban environment in different ways: some see their needs best satisfied by the attributes of central location, others by the new environment of the peripheral residential areas. There is also an indication that willingness to consider and ability to implement a move may be related to such socio-economic characteristics as education and car ownership. Those who are relatively mobile and well informed about the city, and capable of 'working the system', will have more effective freedom of choice than others.

Social segregation in residential space

This brings us to the question of social segregation. Firm evidence of this is hard to find, not least because Soviet society is supposed to be classless and the authorities are reticent about revealing information which might lead to a contrary conclusion. However, various kinds of information are at least suggestive of spatial socio-economic differentiation.

Of particular interest is a further study by Barbash, in which data on the socio-economic structure of the population of different localities within Moscow were compiled as a by-product of an analysis of child health. She selected 24 areas with contrasting environmental quality, and acquired information from the local polyclinics for more than 5000 babies born in 1978. The occupations of the mothers were mapped by 'pie diagrams' according to the following categories: specialists in material production (e.g. engineers, economists and technicians in manufacturing industry), other specialists (e.g. teachers, lecturers, doctors and those working in recreation or scientific research), workers in material production (i.e. manual workers in factories, shops, etc.), students, and others (including housewives and, presumably, the unskilled). The map from the original Russian source is reproduced in Smith (1988, p. 85, Fig. 5.5).

Individual maps showing proportions of mothers in the two specialist categories together and those classified as workers have been compiled by reading approximate figures from the original map. Figure 2.5 shows a tendency towards grouping, some of the highest proportions of workers being in the predominantly industrial south-eastern and eastern wedges of the city. The figures for many of the districts are quite similar, but the proportion of specialists in material production varies from approximately 14 percent to 39 percent and for other specialists from 6 percent to 38 percent (both

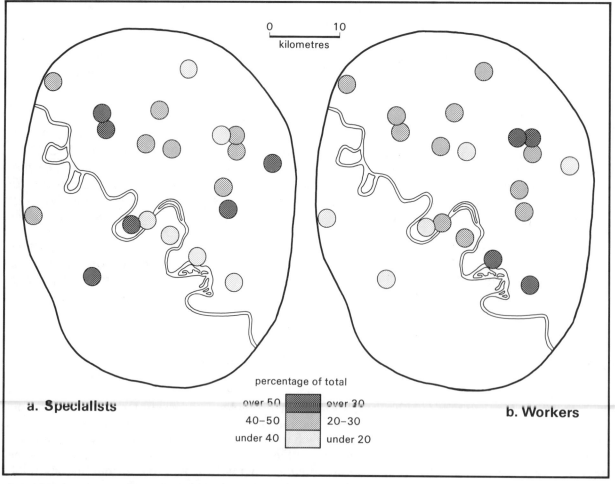

Figure 2.5 Occupational composition of population in selected localities within Moscow, based on mothers of children born in 1978
Source: calculated from original map by N.B. Barbash (in Smith, 1988, p. 85, Fig. 5.5)

groups together range from 20 percent to 56 percent). For proportion of workers the range is 4 percent to 38 percent. For students (not shown in Figure 2.4) it is 4 to 14 percent.

Barbash (1983) found that illness among young children is highest in areas where the proportion of women who are workers (as opposed to specialists) or housewives (single-income households) is greatest, indicating that occupational status as well as local environmental quality can affect other aspects of people's lives.

The elite in Moscow

The 'elite' in Soviet society comprise the upper levels in political, administrative, managerial, military, academic and artistic life. As the capital city of a country with a high degree of central control, Moscow has a disproportionately large share of the elite. In addition to relatively high salaries, they are rewarded by various privileges including access to special facilities providing health care or goods not generally available, for example. They may also be entitled to an additional allocation of housing space and this may be provided in special buildings. In so far as housing for the elite may be concentrated in particular parts of the city, a special kind of social segregation may be found.

*Different generations of housing for the elite in Moscow: **Plate 9** (l) one of the 'Stalin gothic' blocks, reputedly inhabited by leading figures in culture and the arts, among others; **Plate 10** (r) new flats of superior design for 'special people', discretely located close to the city centre.*

Evidence from a variety of sources suggests some spatial concentration of the elite within Moscow. For example, Matthews (in French and Hamilton, 1979, pp.107-8) points to the old aristocratic district of the Arbat in central Moscow being a favourite location for blocks of prestige flats belonging to the Central Committee of the Communist Party and the KGB, and villas built for Party and state leaders on the Lenin Hills (near Moscow State University), as well as new blocks in fairly central locations. French (1987, pp. 313-4) reports: 'Visual inspection on the ground in Moscow suggests that there is a wedge of inner Moscow, within the Garden Ring and running west around the axis of Kalinin Prospect, which contains a high proportion of apartment blocks inhabited by the elite.' Reliable informants have shown the author buildings reputed to be for the elite, including the conspicuous Stalinesque Gothic monuments, pre-Revolutionary blocks built for the bourgeois being renovated from a state of dilapidation or rebuilt behind the original facades, and new blocks which can be distinguished from normal state construction by design and type of brick. While some blocks for the elite seem to be isolated, there are certainly distinct quarters where superior housing and high occupational status go together.

There are also indications of fine *dachas* or country homes outside the city. These are different from the small hut or timber houses which comprise the vast majority of what is claimed to be almost a million *dachas* around Moscow, and probably include some fine pre-Revolutionary palaces. Andrusz (1984, pp. 277-8) suggests that, rather than the suburban living of their Anglo-American counterparts, the Soviet elite prefer to combine a flat near the city centre as permanent residence with a *dacha* often a considerable distance outside the city. Distinct *dacha* communities for the 'high and mighty' were identified in the 1970s by the American journalist Hedrick Smith (see Smith, 1979, p. 240).

Spatial patterns of inequality

The spatial form of socio-economic differentiation or inequality in Moscow suggested by the available evidence may be summarised as follows (Smith, 1988, p. 86). The inner areas present a variety of environments and social groups, with some good housing which combines with access to cultural facilities to generate what may to most people be the best of all worlds in Moscow, other than that of the discreet enclaves of the elite. In contrast, there are the remains of the poor inner-city housing areas, less substantial than in other Soviet cities and occupied by people of markedly lower status than the intelligentsia and 'professional' groups that tend to predominate in the inner city. The outer areas are differentiated by wedges of varying environmental quality and socio-economic status of the population, with the better sectors having relatively high proportions of co-operative housing and the occupations that tend to go with it, the inhabitants trading off higher levels of access to cultural facilities, shopping and other services in the city centre for new housing of good quality and proximity to open space on the edge of the city. In the outer sectors where state housing predominates, environmental quality will be better than in those older, inner areas occupied by people of lower occupational status, except for access to services.

This description suggests elements of both the concentric zone and wedge 'models' of urban spatial structure. The question of which of these two forms predominates in Moscow has exercised the curiosity of a number of observers. S. I. Kabakova, who attempted to estimate 'land values' in the Soviet city, comes up with an almost perfect concentric zone pattern for Moscow (Bater, 1980, 127, Fig. 5). French suggests that at first glance the 'Burgess theory' could have relevance for Moscow, given the street pattern of concentric rings and radials and the concentration of central area functions, but also finds some evidence for the 'Hoyt theory' in the location of industry, the tendency of particular social groups to move outwards in the same sector, and in the planned green wedges (French and Hamilton, 1979, pp. 90-2; French, 1987, pp. 311, 313). The most thorough analysis of the applicability of the two models to Moscow, by Barbash (1982), confirms that one is not obviously more convincing than the other and that it depends on which element of environment, economy or society is considered. Attempts to fit Moscow into one or other of these models is ultimately misguided, however, for they relate to processes of land-use competition which have been substantially modified if not completely eliminated in the socialist city.

Summary

Despite a planning process driven by egalitarian ideals, inequality in living standards is evident in Moscow. Some of this can be attributed to the hierarchical structure of service provision and to the process of physical development over time as well as space. There is also evidence of some spatial sorting of the population by occupational group, including the creation of elite enclaves. With respect to the overall spatial structure of inequality, however, the situation is more complex than the inner/outer distinction which typifies the capitalist city. Socio-economic differentiation certainly exists in Moscow but it appears to be less clearly patterned. Furthermore, Moscow has always had a special status in the Soviet Union, and its uniqueness may provide an insecure basis for generalisation. We shall therefore proceed to the evidence provided by some other Soviet cities.

3. RESIDENTIAL SEGREGATION AND SOCIAL INEQUALITY: EVIDENCE FROM OTHER SOVIET CITIES

This chapter contains three case studies from different kinds of cities, illustrating aspects of residential segregation and associated patterns of social inequality. A brief overview of the evidence with respect to the Soviet city in general is offered by way of conclusion. But first, some background information on urbanisation in the Soviet Union is provided, to set the cases in context.

Urbanisation in the Soviet Union

The Soviet Union is a highly urban society. This is largely the outcome of the socialist era: at the time of the Revolution in 1917, only about 18 percent of the nation's total population of 163 million lived in urban areas compared with two-thirds of a figure approaching 300 million today. Over 112 million lived in cities of 100,000 or more in 1987 compared with about 76 million as recently as 1970, while the number in cities of over a million has doubled during the same period (see Table 3.1).

Table 3.1   Urban population of the USSR 1970-1987

	1970	1979	1987
Total population (million)	242	262	283
Population in urban areas (million)	136	164	188
Number of cities of 100,000 or more	221	273	291
Population of cities of 100,000 or more (million)	76	98	112
Number of cities of 1 million or more	9	18	23
Population of cities of 1 million or more (million)	19	32	41

Source: **Narodnoye Khoziastvo CCCP za 70 let** (Statistical Yearbook of the USSR), Moscow 1987

The proportion of the Soviet population in urban areas is not as high as in most of the advanced capitalist world, where over 80 percent or even 90 percent is not unusual. And it is questionable how much of an 'urban' way of life prevails in many of the smaller places classified as urban. But the figures for cities with a million or more inhabitants indicate that a substantial number of the Soviet people live in metropolitan areas ranging in population from the equivalent of the British cities of Birmingham and Manchester at the lower end of the scale to London, New York and Chicago at the other. Table 3.2 lists the population of the 'millionaire' cities of the USSR. While many of them are not much over the million mark, two exceed 2 million, Leningrad has almost 5 million and Moscow, as officially defined, approaches 9 million.

Table 3.2   Population of the 'millionaire' cities of the USSR 1987 (million)

Moscow	8.815	Novosibirsk	1.423	Cheliabinsk	1.119
Leningrad	4.948	Sverdlovsk	1.331	Alma-Ata	1.108
Kiev	2.544	Kuibyshev	1.280	Ufa	1.092
Tashkent	2.124	Tbilisi	1.194	Donetsk	1.090
Baku	1.741	Dnepropetrovsk	1.182	Perm	1.075
Kharkov	1.587	Ereran	1.168	Kazan	1.068
Minsk	1.543	Odessa	1.141	Rostov	1.004
Gorky	1.425	Omsk	1.134		

Source: **Narodnoye Khoziastvo CCCP za 70 let** (Statistical Yearbook of the USSR), Moscow 1987

Figure 3.1 provides a map of major cities in the Soviet Union. They have been graded according to an index of social infrastructure incorporating information on housing, transportation, retailing and restaurants, public health, education, culture, water supply, sewage services, air pollution and greenery, and the physical setting (for details, see Gomostayeva, 1986). In so far as this index reflects inequalities in living standards among cities, two broad generalisations are suggested. The first is that conditions tend to improve with city size. The second and, perhaps, stronger tendency is for cities in the European part of the country to be better off than elsewhere, especially Soviet Central Asia where the lowest living standards by conventional criteria prevail.

This brief introduction to urbanisation in the Soviet Union at large must suffice for the present purpose. Further background can be found in specialised texts, the most useful being by Bater (1980), Andrusz (1984) and Morton and Stuart (1984), and in various other references cited in this and the previous chapter.

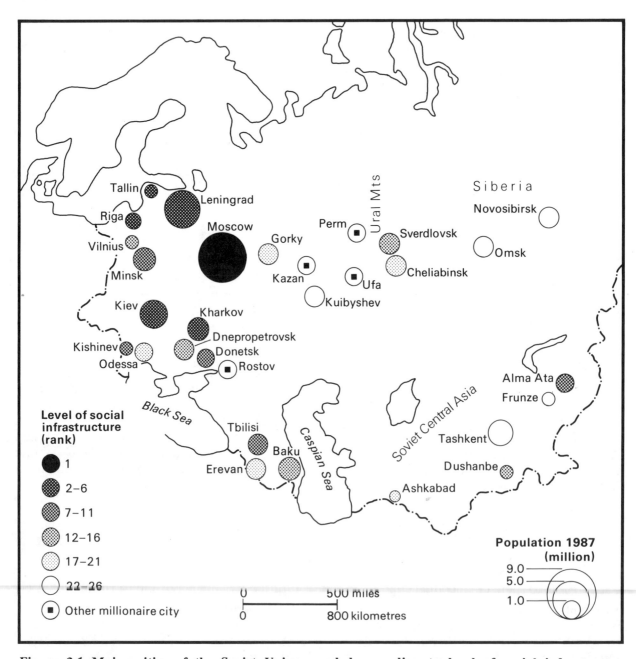

Figure 3.1 Major cities of the Soviet Union, graded according to level of social infrastructure 1978
Sources: populations from **Narodnoye Khoziastvo CCCP** (1987); infrastructure rankings from Gomostayeva (1986, p. 374, Table 1)

Spatial social differentiation: the case of Ufa

Where is Ufa? The fact that probably few readers will have encountered the name Ufa before starting this chapter, never mind being able to locate it on a map, underlines the prevailing degree of ignorance of Soviet cities outside Moscow. Yet Ufa is one of the 'millionaire' cities listed in Table 3.2 above. It happens to be in the Bashkir Autonomous Soviet Socialist Republic, a subdivision of the RSFSR, the existence of which recognises the distinctive character of the Bashkir people. It is on the south-western flanks of the Urals, almost midway between Kuibyshev and Sverdlovsk (Figure 3.1).

The city of Ufa has been introduced not so much to provide an elementary geography lesson as to present some evidence concerning its spatial social differentiation. A study by L.N. Fenin has explored the link between social groups and their location. He provides information on the inhabitants of three types of district: the old centre, the newly constructed areas presumably adjacent to it, and the outer areas characterised by a high proportion of privately owned dwellings with garden plots (Table 3.3).

Table 3.3   The 'social configuration' of districts in Ufa 1968

	Central	New	Outer
Occupational groups (%)			
Workers	33.5	47.1	57.4
Employees (mainly low-grade non-manual)	9.0	17.8	12.2
Intelligentsia (middle- or high-grade technicians)	12.0	10.9	6.2
Intelligentsia (other)	32.4	14.9	11.8
Pensioners	13.1	9.3	12.4
Residents' cultural indices			
Education level (classes completed)	9.9	8.8	7.4
Possessing library, of at least a few books (%)	62.7	53.5	33.1
Possessing garden plot (%)	20.5	11.0	42.4
Possessing domestic animals (%)	6.8	2.3	21.6
Having religious members in family (%)	4.7	9.1	12.0

Source: French and Hamilton (1979, p. 112, Table 5.1)

Some of the indices are open to interpretation: possession of domestic animals may be for protection of property as well as reflecting rural background, and declarations of religious affiliation can hardly have been reliable in the Soviet Union at this time. However, the differences are revealing. M. Matthews summarises the findings as follows (French and Hamilton, 1979, p. 112):

> They suggest that although no district is in any way socially exclusive, there are marked differences between them. Thus the intelligentsia (understood in a broad, Soviet sense [i.e. as people who work with their minds rather than their hands]), better educated, and more 'bookish' folk live more frequently in the centre. The outskirts seem to have a larger share of artisans who are closer to their village antecedents (54 per cent of the inhabitants of the town in 1968-1970 were, it appears, of rural origin). The newly built districts generally come in between.

The author also suggests a gradation of income corresponding with the three types, with the central district leading.

The areas of private housing on the edge of cities like Ufa reflect the pace of urbanisation, and the failure of the local authority to keep up with housing demand via state construction. Private housing is usually of poor quality by conventional standards and may lack such amenities as running water. Local schools may be regarded as inferior by the intelligentsia, because of the predominantly low cultural levels in the home. However, to the migrant from the countryside, these fringe areas combine a first foothold in the city with the ability to supplement uncertain official supply of food from their own plot. And even some flat dwellers may envy the freedom which private housing offers. Thus the quality of life in the outer areas depends very much on individual or family attitudes and values.

Social and ethnic segregation: the case of Kazan

Kazan is the capital of the Tartar Autonomous Soviet Socialist Republic, and is situated roughly midway between Ufa and Gorky (Figure. 3.1). It is the subject of what appears to be the most thorough investigation of the spatial arrangement of population by social status and ethnic origin available for any Soviet city. Rukavishnikov (1978; see Bater, 1984, pp. 152-6 and 1986, pp. 98-9) for summaries) has produced detailed maps for 1974, based on a survey of 3600 people or 0.7 percent of the working population, and also reconstructed features of the city at the turn of the century so that the present (or recent past) can be compared with the pre-Revolutionary patterns.

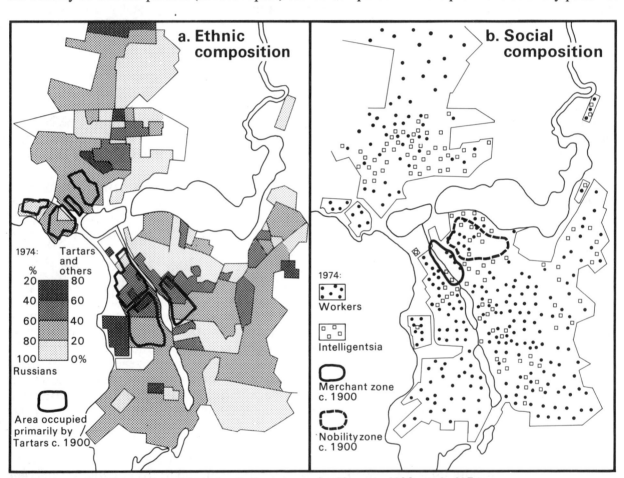

Figure 3.2 Location of social and ethnic groups in Kazan c.1900 and 1974
Source: based on Rukavishnikov (1978, pp. 62 and 70-1, Figs 1, 2 and 3)

Kazan was originally an ethnically homogeneous city populated by Tartars. Russians began to move in as craftsmen, merchants and service gentry when the middle and upper Volga country was annexed by the Russian state in c.1550. The proportion of Russians steadily increased, so that by around 1880 to 1917, when the total population was variously estimated to be 130,000-180,000, Tartars accounted for 15-20 percent. A clear territorial separation of the two ethnic groups could be identified at the turn of the century: the eastern, larger and 'better' part of the city was inhabited by Russians and the western part by Tartars. The areas populated primarily by Tartars are outlined in Figure 3.2a. The minority Russian population in the western (Tartar) part of the city belonged to a comparatively poorer class. It was also possible to identify distinct areas occupied by merchants (about 6 percent of the population) at the intersection of the Tartar and Russian districts, and by the nobility (5 percent) in the Russian district away from the city centre in the higher and more attractive parts of the city. These two areas are outlined in Figure 3.2b. Thus, according to Rukavishnikov (1978, p. 64):

> Prerevolutionary Kazan confirms the well-known proposition that capitalist cities are characterised by settlement in socially and ecologically different parts of the city according to class affiliation. The contrasts of pre revolutionary Kazan were defined not so much by ethnic as social factors, for the conditions of life of the Russian and Tartar proletariat were virtually the same.

Since the Revolution, the population of Kazan has greatly increased, to exceed one million. The proportion of Tartars has also increased, reflecting large-scale migration from the surrounding territory; by the time of the 1974 survey it had reached 31.1 percent, with 64.1 percent Russians and the balance made up of other ethnic groups. Districts with relatively high proportions of Tartars could still be identified, roughly corresponding with those at the turn of the century, as Figure 3.2a shows. But nowhere did Tartars exceed 80 percent of the total population, and they were found to be living in all parts of the city, often side by side with Russians. Rukavishnikov (1978, p. 73) refers to 'the mosaic ethnic structure of socialist Kazan in the 1970s', compared with the more evident segregation of the capitalist city.

As to the social geography of Kazan in the 1970s, revealed by occupational structure, Rukavishnikov (1978, p. 68) summarises the findings as follows:

> No rigid relationship between an individual's status in society and his place of residence is to be found. There are no social groups living solely in the centre of the town or on its outskirts, nor has any social group taken over the ecologically comfortable zones of the city. We were unable to draw boundaries around territorial localizations of individual social strata of citizens or smaller socio-occupational groups, as was done in reconstructing the residential pattern of prerevolutionary Kazan. All that can be seen ... are large regions (in the old downtown districts, for example) where there is a small plurality of white collar and professional people or of workers, but there are no sharp lines of demarcation between such regions, and the social composition within tracts in each region is quite heterogeneous.

Rukavishnikov's original map (reproduced in Bater, 1984, p. 156 and 1986, p. 99) has been simplified in Figure 3.2b by omitting one of the three occupational groups identified (clerical personnel), to highlight the patterns of workers and the intelligentsia (professionals and para-professionals). This suggests a peripheral dominance of workers, and a concentration of professionals in central parts of the city. Some degree of social segregation must therefore be recognised, although the development of the city under socialism has clearly generated more spatial diversity. Distinctive zones which have emerged during the socialist period include 'company' neighbourhoods associated with particular factories, villages enveloped in the expansion of the city, and the fringe areas of 'do-it-yourself' housing occupied by more recent migrants from the countryside.

While high social status and Russian origin are much less closely associated than before the Revolution, there must be some relationship between ethnic group and living conditions in Kazan, because Tartars predominate in the original (and poorer) Tartar parts of the city as well as in the incorporated villages and on the urban fringe. Rukavishnikov (1978, pp. 72 and 74-5) found such a relationship in the industrial city of Al'met'evsk (population about 90,000), with Tartars primarily in zones of old and modern private housing which is usually of inferior quality. And, while 'no localization of social strata exists' here, highly qualified professionals, creative intellectuals and managers were found to live primarily in newly-built areas, presumably of state flats, and in those adjacent to the city centre.

Evidence from other Soviet cities points to continuing ethnic segregation, which might have socio-economic implications. For example, although the major cities of Soviet Central Asia are now predominantly Slavic, many of the indigenous people still prefer to live in traditional quarters,

Samarkand being a case in point (see French and Hamilton, 1979, pp. 145-65 for a discussion of Islamic cities). Distinctive events in the historical treatment of some population groups may also be involved; for example, it is reported that in Alma-Ata, capital of the Kazakh Republic, there is a distinctive area of Turkish and Chechen people (from the northern Caucasus), relocated by Stalin. Initially they were socially deprived, but today their level of living is relatively high due to their activity in the 'second' (alternative or informal) economy. However, they are still concentrated in a relatively poor part of the city in an ecological sense. The crucial issue with respect to ethnic minorities in the Soviet city is the extent to which they chose to live differently, and in different areas from other people, which is not the same as being treated unequally. That certain ethnic groups are dissatisfied with their place in Soviet society, for whatever reason, has been demonstrated recently in Armenia and elsewhere.

Inequality in an academic town: the case of Akademgorodok

The more specialised the function of a city, the more socio-economic homogeneity might be expected. As our final case study of the Soviet city we will take the scientific settlement of Akademgorodok (literally, 'academic township') just outside Novosibirsk in Siberia. The decision to engage in what was heralded as a bold experiment in creating this town was made in 1955, closely associated with the planned development of Siberia. The Siberian Branch of the Soviet Academy of Sciences (the body responsible for administration of scientific research) was set up in 1957 and work on the first institutes and laboratories in Akademgorodok was begun soon afterwards. The town subsequently grew to a population of well over 50,000, housing researchers and others working at 24 scientific institutes, staff and students at the Novosibirsk State University, built here to take advantage of the local concentration of academic talent, and other workers required for the service functions and so on.

The Soviet authorities recognised from the outset that it would not be easy to attract distinguished scientists to Siberia. Most of them were used to the relatively sophisticated life of cities like Moscow along with the privileges of a high-status occupation. There was also the stigma of Siberia's traditional role as a place of exile to overcome. Although only 20 miles from Akademgorodok, the centre of Novosibirsk had a distinctly provincial ambience and restricted range of goods and services available, despite the size of the city. Added to this was the harsh winter. Special measures had therefore to be taken to recruit and maintain first-class scientific personnel in this unlikely and perhaps uninviting location.

The planners began with the advantage of an attractive site, with birch woods sloping down to the shore of the Obskoe More or Ob Sea - a large artificial lake formed by the damming of the River Ob for a hydroelectric project. The town that they built resembles in many respects the urban landscape of the typical post-war Soviet city, with housing and services provided on the *microraion* principle. There is a distinct town centre along Ulitsa Ilicha, with the main service facilities including a hotel, cinema and supermarket (the latter a very rare refinement in the USSR at the time it was constructed). The scientific institutes are ranged along Prospect Nauka, the Science Avenue or Parade. The residential areas with their customary blocks of flats are nearby (Figure. 3.3). But within the urban fabric is a subtle differentiation, or inequality: a reflection of the hierarchical structure of Soviet academic life brought into focus by the small and specialised nature of the town.

At the top of the academic hierarchy are the Academicians, or Members of the Soviet Academy of Sciences. There are about 30 in Akademgorodok, and their status is roughly that of a Fellow of the Royal Society in Britain. Below them are various grades of scientific staff, from chiefs of research groups and sections, through senior research workers and junior research workers, to post-graduate assistants. Anecdotal evidence confirmed from different sources suggests that the normal salary of an Academician, supplemented from lecturing at the University and by special allowances, might be 10 times that of a junior research worker in Akademgorodok. This is roughly twice the range of pay separating staff of comparable status in British academic life. Added to these differentials are the non-pecuniary privileges of elite status, such as access to scarce goods and special services, accorded to those in senior academic positions in the USSR.

As observed in Moscow and other Soviet cities, housing is an important source of inequality. In Akademgorodok there is a recognised and easily discernible distinction between blocks of so-called 'full-size' and 'standard' flats. Scientists with a higher degree such as the doctorate are entitled to extra living space (20 square metres above the norm is a frequently quoted figure, a privilege also enjoyed by certain other professions). Such accommodation may be provided in one of the better blocks, but this appears to depend on the status of the institute in question along with individual seniority, opportunity and the random element of good fortune which can make the difference between whether or not people actually receive their entitlement. Different accommodation again is provided for junior research workers and those who are single, while at the bottom of the qualitative range are student hostels. Some even find rural-type housing outside the town itself. As elsewhere, housing quality appears to vary with period of construction, the earliest blocks in Akademgorodok usually being of the five storeys typical of the Krushchev period, while those of more recent construction are taller, with more balconies, and having some ground-floor shops (quite a convenience in the Siberian winter).

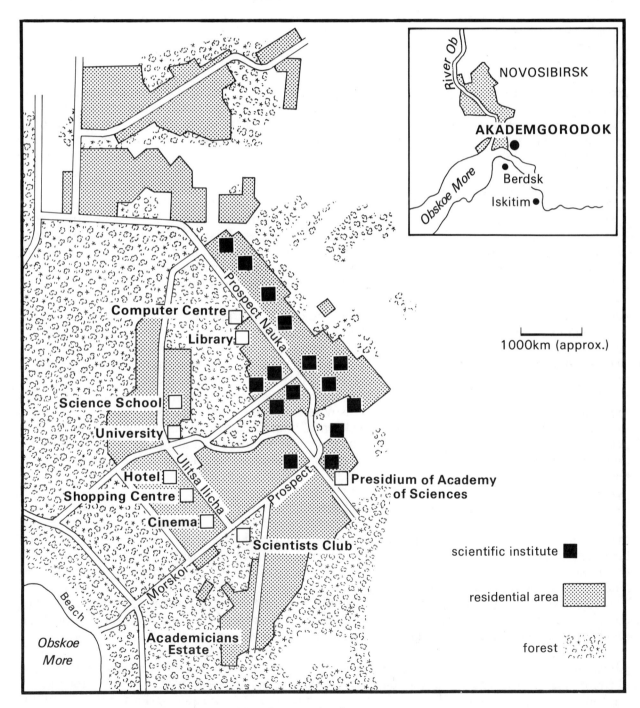

Figure 3.3 Akademgorodok, the Siberian academic town
Source: Smith (1978, p. 241)

*Two types of housing in the Siberian academic town of Akademgorodok: **Plate 11** (l) 'standard' blocks; **Plate 12** (r) 'full-sized' (i.e. better than standard). A place in a better block may depend on status in one of the scientific institutes.*

The greatest and most conspicuous housing privilege is accorded to the Academicians. Their recruitment was crucial to the success of the new science centre, and a small estate of semi-detached and detached single-family homes or 'cottages' was built for them in the southern part of the town (Fig. 3.3). This was described vividly by one of the first western scientific visitors to provide a detailed account of the community, in 1967 (Portisch, 1972, p. 33):

> What did astound me were the outer suburbs, where I found beautiful villas in the midst of the taiga. Virtually all of them were designed for one- or two-family occupation, and certainly did not conform to the standard Soviet norms for the allocation of floor space. These villas were inhabited by scientists, professors and laureates of the Lenin Prize. Some of them were of two storeys and equipped with garages, balconies, terraces and pleasant gardens. The families living in these villas of course had servants - cooks, maids and even butlers. The splendid lawns and flowerbeds were cared for by gardeners employed by the local authority.

Almost two decades later the gardens looked somewhat overgrown, and servants may not be available in such profusion, but there is no doubt that a privileged enclave exists and that there have been additions to the original cottages. Some would not be out of place in wealthier London suburbs. The grandest house, apparently for the Chairman of the Siberian Branch of the Academy, resembles a Swiss chalet and has separate detached quarters for a chauffeur above the garage. One Academician, who was Director of an Institute and is now a senior adviser to President Gorbachev, reputedly preferred not to have a cottage as his wife worked, so two flats were converted into one to give him five rooms. By comparison, the head of a research group was observed to have three generously-sized rooms for his family, a younger research worker had three spartan rooms for the unusually large family of five, and another of comparable status had only two rooms for four people (and had waited some years for this).

In addition to housing privilege there is also differential access to services. For example, there is a well-appointed Scientists' Club or social centre, with meeting rooms, exhibition space, a restaurant serving better food than at the hotel and with less of a wait, and a bar with a more reliable supply of beer (at least on the author's visits). The Academicians have their own small and presumably highly exclusive club house on the edge of their estate. Senior scientists are also entitled to special health-care facilities and to some advantages with respect to the purchase of scarce foodstuffs. There are special English and French schools emphasising the respective languages, with highly competitive entry and reputedly catering largely for children of academic families, as well as schools for those especially gifted in mathematics and certain scientific subjects.

All this is clearly inconsistent with the egalitarian principles upheld in Soviet ideology, even if some of the privileges just described may now have begun to yield to the 'reforms' of Soviet society introduced under Gorbachev. But it is important to recognise that inequality does have a function, as part of a system of incentives and rewards. The opening up of vast natural resources in Siberia, along with strategic considerations, generated a particular national development priority, and with it

Special accommodation for the Academicians (Members of the Soviet Academy of Sciences) in Akademgorodok:
Plate 13 *(l) original semi-detached 'cottage' from the early phase of construction of the town;* **Plate 14** *(r) more recent detached house in the same neighbourhood.*

the need for a regional scientific base. In these special circumstances, special measures were adopted, to make Akademgorodok a special place within which senior scientists would enjoy special privileges. Thus some inequality of living standards is justified by a wider social purpose. Whether the actual degree of inequality is more than required to achieve the desired objective is impossible to say; that it is certainly sufficient is demonstrated by the success of the Siberian science centre.

Inequality in the Soviet city

A Soviet authority has recently commented as follows (Yanitsky, 1986, p. 275):

> In the USSR, intraurban settlement is free from the pressure of socio-economic and racial factors. There are no prestigious social 'oases' or ethnic ghettoes. Public transport is cheap, and the prices of commodities and services are the same throughout the city. When a family is given a new flat, the state (represented by the district Soviet of people's deputies) offers several options of localities. A system of dwellings exchange functions throughout the country. For these reasons, there is no spatial localisation of social or professional groups.

> The choice of residential location is determined by personal preferences, the stage of the family and age cycle, the structure of kinship relationships, as well as differences in the level of development of the social infrastructure in different cities and areas within cities.

It is true that, within the limitations of opportunity, knowledge and bureaucratic inertia, Soviet citizens have more freedom than is often supposed, to seek residential locations within a variable environment, so as to satisfy particular individual or family needs. In so far as different needs are matched by what is available or easily accessible locally, the pattern of living standards as people experience them will tend towards equality. That people freely live differently in different places does not necessarily make them unequal. And there is little if any doubt that, objectively, the Soviet city lacks the stark inequalities of its counterpart under capitalism. But the evidence assembled in this and the previous chapter, along with the broader literature on the Soviet city, clearly reveals Yanitsky's first paragraph as wishful thinking - an expression of official ideology rather than of the reality of the Soviet socialist city.

The following broad typology of socio-economic and environmental differentiation may be suggested, probably represented in most if not all large Soviet cities:

1. *Inner, high-status areas of good housing, occupied largely by the professional groups*: there will be some congestion and pollution, but good access to services accompanies the central location, added to which are the special privileges of those with elite status.

2. *Inner, low-status areas, of old and deteriorating property waiting for renewal:* the environment will be affected by industrial or commercial development, but good access to the facilities of the city centre will provide some compensation.

3. *Outer areas of relatively high status (more or less distant from the centre, depending on the size and growth pattern of the city), with relatively high proportions of co-operative flats:* local employment may be predominantly 'white-collar'; service provision and/or transport to the city centre will be fairly good.

4. *Outer areas of lower status, with a predominance of state housing, and a relatively high proportion of in-migrants; manual employment predominates:* industry has a detrimental environmental impact; access to services is low, and exacerbated by time-lags in construction of the necessary infrastructure.

5. *Peri-urban areas and suburban enclaves of private housing of very poor quality by conventional Soviet standards, much of it occupied by recent migrants from the countryside:* there will be low or non-existent service provision.

6. *Quarters occupied by distinctive ethnic groups, possibly but not necessarily in lower-status occupations:* probably comprising socially cohesive communities; housing may reflect cultural preferences; service provision will depend on position within the general spatial structure of the city.

While housing, occupation and access to the service infrastructure predominate in this typology, there are strong indications that it is reflected in some other social conditions. In health, for example, there is the evidence of Barbash in Moscow cited in the previous chapter. Quality of education is also likely to be associated with local neighbourhood characteristics; R. B. Dobson (Morton and Stuart, 1984, p. 164) comments:

> Schools located in industrial areas have large contingents of working-class children; on the other hand, schools in districts where research institutes and higher educational institutions are concentrated ... have student bodies composed heavily of college educated professionals' children. These variations in the schools' composition in turn affect their quality, for the better qualified teachers are attracted to the 'middle-class' schools.

Social pathologies such as crime, alcoholism and what the Soviets call 'hooliganism' are also associated with particular parts of the city. These tend to be the old and deteriorating neighbourhoods, usually in the central area, and some of the new lower-status residential complexes in the outer districts. The common denominator seems to be a predominance of single rural migrants no longer subject to the traditional controls of family and community (Morton and Stuart, 1984, pp. 122-3; Andrusz, 1984, p. 218; French, 1987, p. 312).

A further element in the social geography of the Soviet city is the tendency for family size to be negatively associated with socio-economic status. The peripheral zones customarily accommodate a younger population with larger average family size (Bater, 1986, p. 94). Spatial sorting may be a response to the differential attraction of particular parts of the city in relation to stage in family life cycle, but there may also be a less voluntary element in population shifts as people are displaced by inner city renewal bringing in those of higher status (Andrusz, 1984, p. 218).

An important question of detail, to which we will return in later chapters, is how far such zones comprise extensive areas of the city with relatively homogeneous character, as opposed to more of a mosaic or patchwork of internal diversity. In Soviet urban planning, any tendency towards social separation and associated bourgeois class attitudes should be prevented by residential mixing, at least by neighbourhood and preferably by residential block. Thus the manual worker and the specialist might live side by side. Firm evidence on the extent to which such mixing has been achieved is rare, but it seems fair to speculate that it is less than the socialist ideal. Nevertheless, Andrusz (1984, p. 220) asserts that, 'Generally speaking however, and with singular exceptions, blocks of flats in the Soviet Union are characterised by social class heterogeneity - certainly by Anglo-American standards'.

French and Hamilton (1979, p. 98) state that social segregation tends to be by building, rather than by street or area. However, this may be true more of the inner than the outer residential areas. Bater (1987, p. 94) suggests that in the new microdistricts and in suburban tracts of individual houses engulfed in the process of urban expansion, 'the social-class composition of particular neighbourhoods is not always as varied as Soviet planning policy suggests it ought to be'. Areas of housing built by industrial enterprises almost inevitably have a working-class character and the tracts of private housing will have a similar composition; higher-status people have other choices, with better housing and environment.

There is certainly some clustering of accommodation for higher-status groups and the elite. Bater (1980, p. 101) suggests that this led to a degree of residential segregation as early as the Stalin era. Concentrations of co-operatives may exist in certain parts of the city, but French (1987, pp. 314-5) points out that the sites for such housing are controlled by the local authority which therefore has the power to prevent spatial clustering of the socio-economic groups that can afford such accommodation. For members of the elite allocated good state housing, apartment size and furnishings may matter more than location (Bater, 1984, p. 149). Even within the prestige blocks built for the elite there can be a degree of mixing; anecdotal evidence indicates that a family can retain a flat originally allocated on the basis of the father's status years after his death, and that some manual workers as well as ballerinas live in Stalinesque Gothic structures. And there is always the chance factor which may enable an enterprising or fortunate individual to take advantage of that uncertain flexibility and inefficiency which is one of the few endearing features of Soviet bureaucracy.

How far inequality in the Soviet city may be affected by the restructuring of Soviet society promoted by Gorbachev, under the banner *perestroika*, is hard to say at this stage. There are indications in recent government decrees on housing of an increasing reliance on the private and co-operation sectors, and of opening up a market in the state sector. There is even the suggestion that rents could be increased in attractive locations. In general, the greater emphasis on personal incentives and the need to supplement state resources by tapping people's savings seem likely to increase the scope for personal spending on housing and environmental quality, along with some other goods and services. Greater inequality in living standards seems a likely outcome, accompanied by further spatial concentration of socio-economic groups. However, the failure of state planning to achieve its objectives is a repetitive feature of Soviet history, and this could be the fate of the new housing policies and other urban reforms.

Conclusion

In view of the imprecision and ambivalence of some of the evidence, the most appropriate conclusion, following Andrusz (1984, p. 220), is that 'It is impossible in Soviet cities to identify ghettos, whether rich or poor: there are only tendencies towards the congregation of social groups'. But as he emphasises throughout his study of the Soviet urban scene, there is an association between housing quality, tenure, social group and spatial location which, along with differentiation of the urban infrastructure, is generating a distinctive kind of city with its own emergent patterns of inequality. How far this is reflected in other East European countries, where there is more direct evidence of both the processes involved and their outcomes, will be examined in the chapters which follow.

4. PRAGUE: THE IMPOSITION OF SOCIALISM

Prague, the capital of Czechoslovakia, has a population of about 1.6 million, which is expected to rise to 2.1 million by the end of the century. The metropolitan region contains 12 percent of the Czech population today, compared with 8 percent in 1930 and 5.5 percent at the turn of the century.

The special interest of Prague is that it provides an illustration of the imposition of a new society onto an inherited urban spatial form. Unlike Moscow, there has not been an attempt to obliterate virtually all the old city. And Prague suffered neither the severe war damage of Budapest nor the almost total destruction of Warsaw. So instead of a simultaneous change of social structure and built form, Prague has seen the formation of socialist society largely on a pre-existing physical and social-ecological structure typical of the European city of industrial capitalism.

In examining the impact of the socialist period, we will be concerned with the mechanisms generating new socio-economic patterns. As we have seen in Moscow, the traditional 'models' or 'theories' associated with patterns of concentric rings or wedges do little if anything to explain urban form under socialism, for they depend on a process of competition for land which is part of capitalist economy and society. To quote Musil (1987, p. 27):

> The economic models normally used for the explanation of empirical findings about the socio spatial structure of cities are irrelevant in socialist countries, where market mechanisms are almost abolished, or substantially limited. They have to be replaced by other explanations, which are, however, as yet not satisfactorily developed, verified, and formalised. Generally, it is agreed that such procedures should be based to a lesser extent on economic paradigms and more on a knowledge of the sociopolitical, planning and legal mechanisms which allocate the population and social strata within the housing stock and in urban space, and which have replaced market forces as the means of distribution.

The case of Prague enables us to open up these issues, discussion of which will continue in subsequent chapters. Prague was the first major East European city to be the subject of thorough ecological investigation after the advent of socialism (Musil, 1968). This study has been followed up by other Czech scholars, whose findings have been presented and debated in a much more open manner than normally characterises Soviet urban analysis. Thus we should be able to begin to penetrate processes here which remain largely obscured in the USSR. Our discussion will be confined to the single city of Prague, but broader background on urban development in Czechoslovakia will be found in Musil and Rysavy (1983).

Pre-socialist Prague

The main body of this chapter is based on a comparison of the social-ecological structure of the city of Prague in 1930 and 1970, undertaken by Mateju, Vecernik and Jerabek (1979). Information was compiled for 45 districts, on 15 variables chosen so as to be closely comparable for the two years. The variables were mainly measures of housing conditions, occupation and other attributes of socio-economic status. The data were used to produce typologies of Prague's spatial units in 1930 and 1970. These are illustrated in Figure 4.1.

The pattern for 1930 revealed three fairly distinct concentric zones, comprising (1) the city centre, (2) an intermediate residential zone, and (3) the outer residential zone. These may be subdivided into five types, as follows:

I   The predominantly petty-bourgeois inner city residential area associated with the commercial and historic core.

II   A socially mixed residential area linked with large industrial concentrations.

III An emerging residential district of bourgeoisie and clerks in the north-western sector.

IVA Less urbanised socially mixed districts of the outer residential zone.

IVB Predominantly working-class quarters of the outer zone, with lowest socio-economic levels.

Some of the differences between these types of area are indicated in Table 4.1. The proportion of working class in the economically active population was markedly higher in types IVA and IVB, with the figures for I and II markedly lower than elsewhere. Proportion of dwellings with a bathroom was very low in IVB, less than a third of the figure for III, with the other three types in between. Density of occupation again showed the outer working-class areas (IVB) to be worst, with the inner city (I) joining the new well-to-do suburbs (III) as best off. The final column of the table shows a composite indicator of socio-economic level, suggesting a sharp distinction between the best-off type III, the worst-off type IVB, and the other three with similar intermediate levels.

These data, along with the map (Figure. 4.1a), suggest a strongly spatially differentiated city. As Musil (1987, p. 29) describes it:

> Prague of the thirties had all the characteristics of other fast growing metropolises of western capitalist countries. In this period, the social-class differentiation of the society dominated Prague's social ecology and was manifest in the spatial separation of social classes, eg in the segregation of the working class and in a clear differentiation of the various social classes' housing and environmental conditions.

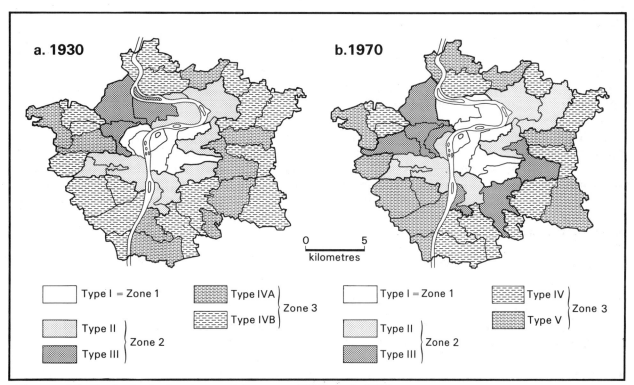

Figure 4.1 Ecological structure of Prague 1930 and 1970
Source: Mateju, Vecernik and Jerabek (1979, pp. 185 and 187, Figs 1 and 2)

Mateju, Vecernik and Jarabek (1979, p. 190) saw an intensification of segregation during the inter-war period:

> The once socially heterogeneous districts were gradually becoming homogeneous, due to their dependence upon the character of existing or constructed housing stock. The urban fringes were becoming proletarian, while wealthy strata tended to retreat from the centre of the city and from the industrial areas of the intermediate zone into newly built residential quarters. The city's centre was inhabited by the petty bourgeoisie, clerks and the working-class aristocracy.

It was on to this social geography of the typical capitalist city that a new social order was to be imposed.

Table 4.1 Indicators of Prague's social ecology in 1930

Type of area	Working class in active population (%)	Dwellings with bathroom (%)	Persons per room	Socio-economic level
I	27.9	30.9	1.24	+0.129
II	41.4	28.4	1.61	-0.142
III	27.8	55.2	1.18	+1.843
IVA	50.4	27.0	1.62	+0.175
IVB	61.7	16.3	1.91	-1.099
max:min	1.18	3.39	1.62	

Source: Mateju, Vecernik and Jerabek (1979, p. 186, Table 1)

Socialist Prague

The early years of the socialist period, from the Second World War to the latter part of the 1950s, was characterised largely by the redistribution of the existing housing stock according to new criteria of need. This favoured the working class, who were able to move into accommodation not previously available. There was thus an evening out of geographical differences, with the proportion of manual workers in the inner zones increasing to about 40 percent in 1961 compared with little over a quarter in 1930 (Musil, 1987, p. 31).

The 1960s saw the beginning of a phase of accelerated housing construction, which continued through the 1970s. Large estates were built on the fringe of the city, to relieve congestion on the centre and facilitate reconstruction of the inner areas as well as to accommodate the growing workforce. The social ecology identified in 1970, reflecting the first part of this phase, is shown in Figure 4.1b. A pattern of concentric zones similar to those in 1930 can be observed, but with significant changes in the character of various parts of the city. The five types of areas now recognised are as follows:

I   An expanded central zone less differentiated from the rest of the city than in 1930.

II   Areas associated with the industrial concentrations, which had been acquiring a working-class character in the pre-war years, now aging in both material structure and population; with certain parts of the centre, these areas show the greatest discrepancy between inherited structures and society's new value and needs.

III Areas better than average in terms of material structure, with above-average proportions of people with higher education and the lowest proportion of workers. Some of these areas had thus preserved their relatively high status of 40 years before.

IV   New housing estates built predominantly in the 1960s.

V   Stagnating districts of the outer zone where both material conditions and social characteristics have remained relatively unchanged. They were being transformed into type IV by the construction of housing estates alongside former family housing areas.

Table 4.2 shows that differences between the five types of areas could still be identified, most obviously the markedly higher proportion of the working class in type V and the low proportion of dwelling with a bath there and, to a lesser extent in type II. However, the differences are much smaller than in 1930 (Table 4.1), as can be seen by comparing the ratios of maximum to minimum values as a simple measure of degree of inequality.

Table 4.2 Indicators of Prague's social ecology in 1970

Type of area	Working class in active population (%)	Dwellings with bathroom (%)	Persons per room	Socio-economic level
I	40.1	75.6	1.09	+0.146
II	46.9	60.4	1.12	-0.618
III	37.3	80.4	1.05	+0.784
IV	40.9	86.1	0.98	+0.485
V	52.9	50.9	1.10	-0.238
max:min	1.14	1.69	1.14	

Source: Mateju, Vecernik and Jerabek (1979, p. 188, Table 2)

The socio-economic (or class) structure had become much less important in the spatial differentiation of Prague. More significant in 1970 was the material or physical quality of the urban environment, with a distinction between the old, obsolescent parts of the city and the newly developed areas, along with family and age structure (Mateju, Vecernik and Jerabek, 1979, pp. 192-3; Musil, 1987, pp. 32-3). A process of homogenisation of urban space had been set in motion, in the interest of social equality; but at this point in the transition to the socialist city there was still spatial differentiation arising from the inherited built environment, its variability, and how it compared with new construction. And there was a social dimension to this differentiation. Just as the type III areas still had a relatively high-status population, so old people with a lower social position were the only ones who remained voluntarily in the poor and overcrowded housing of type II. The greatest social heterogeneity was found in the new outer suburbs (type IV), where housing was allocated to families on the basis of need.

The new process of differentiation

We will now bring the discussion up to date, in an attempt to identify the spatial form that has subsequently emerged and the process behind it. The emphasis will be very much on housing, for it is largely in access to accommodation of different quality and associated environmental attributes that opportunities for differentiation arise.

The four basic types of housing in Czechoslovakia are the same as in the Soviet Union: state, enterprise, co-operative and private. State and enterprise housing is financed from public funds and provided at a rent less than the cost of construction and maintenance. Co-operative housing depends on private funds along with a state grant and low-interest loan, while private housing is mainly financed from personal resources with some state assistance. Herein lies an important distinction: the housing expense of those in co-operatives and new private housing are considerably higher than in state housing, and the difference has been growing (Musil, 1987, p. 28).

During the socialist period, state housing construction has been closely linked to industrialisation, ensuring the availability of accommodation at low cost and in the right place especially to low-income families. Private building was seen as a means of improving the housing situation on the basis of the voluntary contribution of people's own money and labour. The smallest scope for the exercise of consumer needs and preferences is in the state sector, while the greatest is in construction or purchase of an individual house. Individuals can also seek to exercise choice through the exchange of flats as well as acquisition of private housing. The ecological structure of Czech cities is thus the outcome of an interplay between central planning and individual volition.

Following the initial phase of housing redistribution and that of large-scale construction, a third phase may be identified, after 1980. This has been characterised by emphasis on qualitative aspects of housing and environment, and by growing differentiation of the old and new parts of Prague. Musil (1987, pp. 34-5) describes it as follows:

Over the last 10 years the proportion of individual housing construction, i.e. private house-building, has increased in Prague, as well as the proportion of cooperative house-building of small and low-rise complexes These are usually situated outside the big housing estates, being relatively small and frequently not registered as separate statistical territorial units. In addition, they seem to emphasise by their character the top quality locations as regards environmental conditions and are situated in the traditionally preferred localities which have already in the past attracted 'better housing'. The available data and information show that the owners of these dwellings are neither socially exclusive nor apparently homogeneous. But, these territories are populated by households which do have some characteristics in common. This new homogeneity can be described as similar or even identical accessibility of the so-called sources of good housing.

Those attributes which facilitate access to better quality housing are occupational status (top specialists, artists, etc.), high income, and the ability to reduce construction costs along with information about available plots and so on.

According to Musil, the better quality housing is now dispersed, unlike that of the pre-socialist period. And in the new housing estates, state, enterprise and co-operative blocks of flats are mixed. Thus, Musil (1987, p. 35) sees 'an increase of heterogeneity in macrostructure', accompanied by 'a certain homogenization which contributes to the emergence of problem areas' occupied by old people and less qualified workers in the inner districts and some older industrial parts of the city. However, Szelenyi (1987, p. 5) takes issue with these findings, claiming that the failure to identify a strong association between occupational stratification and social segregation arises from methodological problems. In other words, Szelenyi sees the socialist city differentiated by broad zones, as he found in Hungary (see Chapter 5) whereas Musil's claim is that Prague comprises more of a patchwork.

Summary

The inherited built form of the capitalist city has had an important bearing on the changing social geography of the city during the socialist period. To quote Musil (1987, p. 32) once again:

> even an extensive house building programme carried out in the sixties - and, it may be added, even in the seventies - combined with many other deep social changes, were not able to completely transform the inherited features of Prague's social ecology. The inner parts of the city did not essentially change and the traditional attraction of certain districts for certain social groups remained rather strong. Also the inherited location of industrial as well as non-industrial workplaces undoubtedly played an important role in shaping the ecological pattern of the city.

The socialist period expanded the city, creating new residential areas of relatively uniform quality, at least with respect to state housing, but much of the old city has remained. The districts of poor housing and low environmental quality invite renewal, or perhaps revitalisation if in otherwise attractive inner city locations, but it is hard to justify the elimination of sound housing in such areas as long as there is shortage. Access to existing housing of varied quality, along with the freedom of those with the means and ability to build or acquire private housing or join a co-operative, provides ample scope for people to become unequal, in terms of their accommodation and the local environment which goes with it.

How far the advantages accrue to high-status occupational groups is unclear. Relatively high incomes must be a necessary condition for co-operative living and private purchase, if not always construction (building workers should have the edge over professionals here). Nor is it clear how far and at what scale housing quality is associated with occupational status in creating spatial segregation in Prague. More detailed research is required for further exploration of these issues in Czechoslovakia. Meanwhile, we will turn to cities in other countries to see what light they can shed on what we are discovering is an increasingly intricate process.

5. HOUSING DISTRIBUTION: THE EXPERIENCE OF HUNGARIAN CITIES

It will be clear by now that the spatial form of the socialist city depends to some extent on the country in question. In moving to Hungary we encounter a society which, although socialist, differs in significant respects from the Soviet Union and Czechoslovakia. It has experienced what are generally referred to as 'reforms', frustrated in Czechoslovakia after the demise of the so-called 'Prague spring' in 1968 when there was an attempt to establish 'socialism with a human face' and only recently contemplated in the USSR under Gorbachev's *perestroika*. By comparison, the Hungarian economy and society has for some time been less centrally controlled.

There is also an important difference in housing characteristics, a matter which we are discovering to be vital to patterns of inequality. About three-quarters of Hungarian housing is privately owned. This is much higher than the one-quarter in the USSR, and higher even than in Britain (roughly half) and such other West European countries as Sweden and West Germany (both about a third private). High private home ownership is typical of the Balkans, where socialist Bulgaria and Yugoslavia both have about 70 percent, as does Greece. This is a feature of pre-socialist society which has survived the change in social-political system, albeit in a new institutional context. We shall see something of its significance in this chapter.

The population of Hungary's capital, Budapest, along with the five major regional centres, is shown in Table 5.1. Here is a case of what is sometimes termed 'extreme primacy', with the largest city dominating the rest to the extent of having 10 times the population of the second city. Historically, Budapest's share of the national population has grown steadily, to reach about 20 percent today.

We shall begin not with Budapest but with the two regional centres of Pecs and Szeged, subject of a particularly influential study in the late 1960s. Some aspects of changing housing policy will then be reviewed, before concluding with a look at the capital. Background on broader aspects of urbanisation in Hungary can be found in Danta (1987) and Zovanyi (1986).

Table 5.1 Population of major cities in Hungary 1900-1985 ('000s)

City	1900	1920	1949	1960	1970	1980	1985
Budapest	716	929	1590	1805	2001	2060	2074
Miskolc	41	57	109	144	181	207	212
Debrecen	72	103	111	130	162	192	210
Szeged	100	119	87	99	152	171	180
Pecs	42	48	88	115	150	169	176
Gyor	28	50	58	84	103	124	130

Sources: Zovanyi (1986); **United Nations Demographic Yearbook**, 1986

Pecs and Szeged

These two regional centres are the subject of one of the most thorough investigations of housing inequality under socialism yet to be undertaken. In 1968 the Hungarian sociologists G. Konrad and I. Szelenyi carried out a survey involving 2300 families in the cities of Pecs and Szeged, to find out whether a new pattern of urban inequality could be detected under socialism. In particular, they sought to reveal how the unequal distribution of social privileges and disadvantages arising from the differentiation of socialist society was related to the spatial distribution and mobility of the social groups concerned. The account which follows is based on Szelenyi (1983).

Taking the concept of 'housing classes', or position in the housing system, from the literature of western urban sociology, Szelenyi (1983, pp. 49-51) identified the following housing class structure for Hungary in the latter part of the 1960s:

1. Tenants of new state apartments, built to high standards and at high cost, and also of the best pre-war apartments nationalised by the state; allocated at very low rents, this housing carried the largest state subsidies.

2. Tenants of old state-owned flats of lower quality, most of them in single-storey buildings; although available on the same terms as the new housing, the poor quality and maintainence of this property means that it carried comparatively little subsidy.

3. Owner-occupiers of bank-financed and co-operative apartments and villas with private gardens, the best housing outside the state sector; the financing of this property with state assistance provided a significant subsidy.

4. Builders of new family houses, the best of the privately-owned stock of this kind; carried little subsidy.

5. Owners of old family housing, mostly of fairly primitive 'village' character; carried no subsidy.

6. People without houses or flats of their own, living with parents, in rented rooms or other sub-tenancies, or in institutional accommodation, and accounting for about 10% of urban families.

The first two categories refer to the 'state' sector, the next three to the 'market' sector.

The allocation of occupational groups among different kinds of housing is shown in Table 5.2. Family housing is grouped together here, and those in private housing owned by someone else are omitted. There is a striking distinction between the relatively high proportions of bureaucrats, intellectuals, technicians and clerical workers in first-class state housing and the lower proportions of skilled, semi-skilled and unskilled workers. The same distinction is shown for those with their own bank-financed or co-operative apartment. For family housing, however, the proportions of bureaucrats and intellectuals are low; the figure rises steadily from the technicians, clerical, service and skilled workers, through the semi-skilled, to the unskilled. In general, the higher-status groups received the better housing, with the highest subsidies. Szelenyi (1983, p. 56) claimed similar outcomes in other socialist country, concluding: 'It is inherent in the housing economy of the East European countries that people with higher qualifications and incomes will systematically obtain large shares of the housing in new state-owned apartment buildings'.

Table 5.2   Housing type of occupational groups in Pecs and Szeged 1968

Occupational status	% with first-class state housing	% with other state housing	% with own bank-financed or co-op apartment	% with own family house
High bureaucrats	48	10	16	18
Intellectuals	50	11	16	13
Technicians	37	9	11	32
Clerical workers	46	5	6	29
Service workers	38	7	6	27
Skilled workers	25	12	8	28
Semi-skilled workers	24	12	4	40
Unskilled workers	23	10	2	49
Agricultural workers	3	3	0	89
Retired intellectuals	46	5	6	26
Retired workers	22	7	2	46

Source: Szelenyi (1983, p. 53, Table 2.3); percentages in original rounded

How did these disparities arise? Szelenyi (1983, pp. 58-9) identified the manner in which his Pecs and Szeged sample had acquired their housing. Those who had been awarded state housing included 37 percent of the high bureaucrats and almost 40 percent of intellectuals, compared with figures of about 25 percent to 21 percent for skilled, semi-skilled and unskilled workers. The situation was reversed for those who had built or bought their own houses, however, with only about 26 percent of bureaucrats and 21 percent of intellectuals in this category compared with about 35 percent of skilled and semi-skilled workers and 44 percent of the unskilled. These distinctions were reflected in the cost of accommodation; the higher occupation groups systematically paid less than the others, if anything at all.

Szelenyi (1983, p. 63) summarised the trends as follows:

the social groups with highest incomes move steadily towards the highest housing classes in the state and market sectors, and come close to monopolising them. Below that, the highest class of housing available to most of those with lower incomes is the second market class, i.e. the range of family houses omitting the superior 'villa' category. The housing options and opportunities of these lower classes are limited more by state policies which allocate state housing and credit than by the people's capacity to pay. Public policy thus provides that, on average, the richer classes get better housing for less money and effort, while the poorer classes get worse housing at the cost of more money or effort, or both.

So, whereas under socialism housing is supposed to have a special significance as an equalising element of state provision received as a right not as a reflection of income, it was found to be a source of inequality compounding other inequalities arising from occupational status.

Szelenyi went on to consider the ecological structure of the two cities, to see whether there was any correspondence between the physical and functional characteristics of areas and their demographic and social composition. The following zones were identified on the basis largely of housing stock along with economic and institutional functions (Szelenyi, 1983, pp. 108-11):

1. The city centre, containing institutions satisfying city-wide needs, along with nearby residential areas mainly of terraced houses of several storeys.

2. The transitional zone, between the centre and the modern industrial and residential areas, with mixed building forms including detached and semi-detached housing and some terraces as well as industrial and commercial uses. This zone is divided into a transitional zone I with good family housing and apartments, and a transitional zone II with old, poor and deteriorating housing of village style and single-storey multi-flat structures.

3. Mixed industrial-residential areas, originating from the turn of the century, with family houses of the 1920s and estates of the 1950s.

4. New multi-storey housing estates, usually state-owned and of good quality with full urban services.

5. Outer suburbs of family houses, comprising single-storey dwellings with private gardens and of variable quality: some parts will be truly suburban with villa-style housing, while others will be more village-style and poorly serviced. Some parts date from the pre-socialist period, while others include housing built more recently.

Szelenyi did not include maps in his study, but the general form suggested is sketched out in Figure 5.1.

Table 5.3 confirms the predominant housing characteristics of the zones. The multi-storey housing varied with age, that of better quality being generally the post-war construction. Similarly, the standard of the family housing was variable. The single-storey apartments tended to be of poor quality.

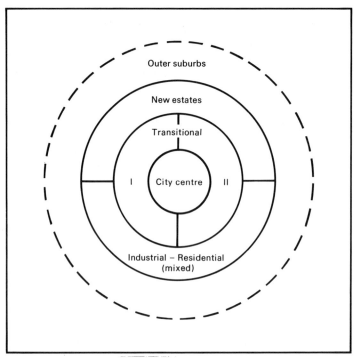

Figure 5.1 Housing zones of Hungarian cities at the end of the 1960s
Source: suggested by Szelenyi (1983, pp. 108-11)

Table 5.3 Housing characteristics of zones of Pecs and Szeged 1968

Zone	% of all city dwellings in zone which are:			% of zone's dwellings built after 1945
	multi-storey houses or flats	single-storey apartment houses	single-storey family houses	
City centre	69	22	9	21
Transitional I	38	31	30	25
Transitional II	18	46	36	13
Mixed	22	35	43	26
New estates	100	0	0	100
Outer suburbs	7	14	79	36

Source: Szelenyi (1983, pp. 111-12, Tables 5.1 and 5.2); percentages rounded

Table 5.4 Housing facilities by zone in Pecs and Szeged 1968

Zone	% with bathroom and all facilities	% with water, gas and electricity	% without piped water
City centre	61	68	12
Transitional I	62	32	13
Transitional II	33	10	55
Mixed	41	8	50
New estates	98	97	0
Outer suburbs	48	3	49

Source: Szelenyi (1983, pp. 114-15, Tables 5.3-5.5); percentages rounded

The qualitative distinctions between housing in the different zones are underlined in Table 5.4. In the new estates, modern facilities are virtually ubiquitous. Overall the city centre is next well served, with the lowest levels in the poorer transitional zone, the mixed industrial-residential areas and the outer suburbs. There is a marked contrast in the availability of piped water, some zones having around half without, while for the others it is not much more than 10 percent.

The extent of occupational segregation by zones is shown in Table 5.5. Relatively high proportions of intellectuals, other white-collar workers and skilled blue-collar workers lived in the new multi-storey housing estates, with correspondingly lower proportions of the professionals in the transitional II, mixed and outer zones. Unskilled workers made up more than half the households in these zones of poorer housing, with only 18 percent in the new state housing areas.

Table 5.5 Occupations of heads of households (% of total) by zones in Pecs and Szeged 1968

Zone	Intellectuals	Other white-collar workers	Skilled blue-collar workers	Unskilled blue-collar workers
City centre	17	31	20	32
Transitional I	15	25	20	40
Transitional II	6	17	26	51
Mixed	4	14	27	55
New estates	23	28	31	18
Outer suburbs	4	16	26	54

Source: Szelenyi (1983, p. 116, Table 5.7); percentages rounded

Szelenyi (1983, p. 117) concluded as follows:

> the degree of segregation of our cities is measurable. It is also clear that all the measured social and spatial advantages tend to be superimposed on one another to increase the privilege of the privileged, while the corresponding disadvantages go together to worsen the situation of the disadvantaged. The higher social classes with the higher status and the better educational qualifications are situated in the better zones of the city; the lower social classes with lower status and less education tend to live in the poorer zones.

Furthermore, those with low incomes who got poor housing in poor districts typically paid more for it than the richer people paid for better housing in better districts. State housing allocation favoured those of high status, the workers seeking new accommodation largely being forced out of the city to build for themselves.

Changing housing policy

The situation identified by Szelenyi applied to a distinctive phase in the development of housing policy in Hungary. It generated a distinctive pattern of urban inequality. We will now review the way in which policy has changed, and its implications for inequality with respect both to quality of housing and what people pay for it. Of particular importance in Hungary is the distinction between state and private provision and the role each plays in the process of equalisation (or otherwise).

As elsewhere in Eastern Europe, the first phase in housing policy under socialism comprised repair of stock damaged in the war, along with some redistribution. Larger houses originally occupied by the bourgeoisie were subdivided and reallocated, yet it is hard to say just how egalitarian this process was. The old capitalist system of inequalities may merely have been replaced by new inequalities: 'the best bourgeois housing went to the new cadre intelligentsia, to the top party and state bureaucrats, high ranking officers in the army, and security forces' (Szelenyi, 1987, p. 2). Industrial reconstruction required accommodation of labour where it was needed, however, and this pragmatic consideration as well as egalitarian ideals must have geared the process of redistribution towards the working class.

The next phase was essentially that described in Pecs and Szeged, with the first state housing constructions. A sharp distinction appeared during the 1960s between the state and non-state (private or market) spheres, with the state supplying relatively high-value, good-quality housing with large subsidies, but in such short supply that many people had to resort to self-building or purchase in the market sphere where housing was predominantly of low value and quality, and with little or no state subsidy. That this situation increased inequality is generally agreed; the two sources of inequality, in consumption and price or subsidy, coincided (Hegedus, 1988, p. 130). This phase had a spatial expression: family houses were built on the outskirts of the cities or in the villages, while inside the city was the domain of state housing.

The beginning of the 1970s saw the introduction of new policies, with a 15-year plan to build a million dwellings. Having created the necessary construction industry, the state set about producing a large volume of flats with the emphasis on quantity rather than size or quality. Most were in high-rise prefabricated blocks. A new Housing Act in 1971 strengthened the welfare role of state housing, and the basis for distribution of the new stock shifted from occupational privilege of the kind described by Szelenyi to criteria of need such as family size and resources. That this led to a decrease in housing inequalities is unquestionable (Tosics, 1988, p. 134). For example, Hegedus (1987, p. 83) shows that in two middle-sized cities in the second half of the 1970s the proportion of managers and professionals in public rental housing was around 30 percent while for semi-skilled workers it was 40 percent, and 66 percent for the unskilled - a striking contrast with Szelenyi's findings for the 1960s reported above.

The interpretation of this phase as egalitarian is not completely straightforward, however. Sillince (1985a, pp. 306-9) has produced evidence that the better-off, high-status groups were still receiving more subsidy and better housing from the state in the 1970s; the reforms had not fundamentally reduced their advantage, although the poorest and most needy groups had been given greater access to low-quality state housing.

The role of the private or market sector is another source of complication. One aim of the reforms initiated at the beginning of the 1970s was to encourage people to solve their own housing problems privately. The expansion of state-subsidised mortgages boosted construction of private houses and flats. There is an argument that, as this attracted more of the well-to-do into a sector previously largely the province of the poor, it made state housing more accessible to those most in need (e.g. Szelenyi, 1987, p. 4). The effect of private sector growth might thus have been egalitarian. However, expansion of private housing could have benefited the richer groups more than the poor; many of the former used state subsidised mortgages while the latter had to rely almost exclusively on their own resources. Hegedus (1987, p. 86) concludes that the state and market processes both contributed to inequality; in the two middle-sized cities which he studied, those with larger incomes, more schooling, some wealth and higher consumption levels got better housing in both the state and market spheres.

Policy changed again in the early 1980s, prompted in part by limitations on state finance. The emphasis shifted from the production of rented dwellings to private provision, along with a levelling out of financial assistance, and hence price, for different forms of housing. The impact on (in)equality is, again, ambiguous. As Tosics (1987, p. 71) puts it:

> the modification of housing policy succeeded in preventing a drastic reduction in housebuilding: many more of the population than before were drawn into the financing of housing by subsidies which were reduced in volume but which were more evenly distributed among the different housing forms. But, also, privatization led to a reduction in the absolute number of social dwellings which has had a negative influence upon the inequalities in housing consumption which exist between different social strata and groups.

Thus the coincidence of inequalities in consumption (or quality) of housing in the 1960s, modified but perhaps not fundamentally altered in the 1970s, has now changed significantly: subsidies are more evenly distributed, though arguably still favouring the well-to-do in relative terms, while marked differences in housing quality among groups in Hungarian society remain and may be increasing.

The new emphasis on privatisation in housing has stimulated a debate on the relative merits of state and market provision. On the one side it is argued that privatisation has a positive effect in reducing the role of ineffective state bureaucracy, and at the same time helps to compensate for inequalities caused by the state; thus the larger the role of the market the more equality in the housing system. On the other side, it is asserted that market processes increase tension between different income groups and require state intervention to aid the poor; the expansion of the market sector means that the lower social strata will have less access to better housing. The evidence from Hungary, examined by Hegedus (1987, pp. 90-91) and others seems ambiguous. The state housing system certainly assists those in need to get housing, but it also produces inequalities that tend to reflect social status. However, private provision by the market also generates inequalities, and its growth can divert state attention as well as resources from those most in need. How far both sectors can be manipulated by the privileged for their own ends depends ultimately on the role of the state, which facilitates and controls the private market sector as an integral feature of 'socialist' society.

Housing and social segregation in Budapest

While subject to the same general policies as the country at large, Budapest does have some distinctive features; in particular, the housing situation is significantly different from the rest of the country, with only one-third private ownership in the city. The metropolis, with a population of about 1.4 million, may be divided broadly into the inner city with its commercial and older residential quarters, the suburban belt of settlements attached administratively to Budapest in 1950, and an outer ring of villages and small towns lying within 10-15 km of the city boundary and linked with Budapest for planning purposes.

Budapest suffered considerable damage during the Second World War, and the years 1946-49 were preoccupied with reconstruction or repair of dwellings along with factories and the urban infrastructure. Some subdivision of housing took place, and redistribution was accelerated when the Communist Party took over in 1948-49. Its rapidly expanding administrative staff, coming from rural areas or at least from lower housing classes, gradually occupied the best-quality dwellings in the best positions (Hegedus and Tosics, 1983, pp. 475-6.) Further redistribution took place as other people engaged in spontaneous occupations which were legitimised by the authorities, and as institutions took over property mainly for their own members.

Despite its importance to the national economy, there were attempts to restrict the growth of Budapest in the 1950s. This exacerbated the housing shortage, which was compounded by poor quality and lack of amenities within the existing stock. At the end of the decade, plans were drawn up to build 250,000 new dwellings in the city, 80 percent of them from public funds. However, the national economy could not support this level of activity and official prejudice against the private sector was relaxed so that, in the 1960s and 1970s, 30-40 percent of construction in the capital came from private building. Pressure on land for industry and other uses had led to prohibitions on private building in large areas and, in any event, the single-family structures which predominated were viewed as an inefficient use of scarce building resources. Multi-family construction was therefore encouraged in private development.

As nationally, the public housing programme in Budapest was boosted by the initiation of prefabricated construction. The new high-rise estates required relatively open areas, and these were largely found between the densely built city centre and the suburban settlements annexed in 1950. It was these dwellings which were the subject of the new allocation criteria favouring large families: predominantly the working class.

A process of spatial sorting of the population was taking place, associated with growing polarisation of housing classes. This may be summarised thus (following Hegedus and Tosics, 1983, pp. 483 and 489). In the early stages the housing stock of the outer city (where private building had been prohibited) and of the unreconstructed inner city suffered relatively rapid deterioration, while new housing areas came into being as the inner ring of new public estates and the zones of multi-family private housing. Later, the high-rise estates began to serve as an intermediate stage in the working-class move out to single-family houses in the suburbs or the agglomeration belt beyond. For those of higher status, now excluded from cheap state housing, the most favourable prospect is high-rise private estates of better than average quality and in relatively good locations. The very best housing remains the high-quality single-family and multi-family blocks of the traditional residential districts. The most obsolete and run-down area is between the inner city and the estates.

While the 1970s had seen a reassertion of criteria of social need in housing distribution compared with the 1960s, Hegedus and Tosics (1983, p. 491) found this not to be reflected in a moderation of segregational tendencies:

> Research in urban sociology in the 1970s demonstrated a significant segregation of the different layers of society: 62 percent of the dwellings of good ecological circumstances were occupied by active or pensionable intellectuals, while their share in single-family houses in the outer districts of the city and in the lowest housing classes (the industrial parts of the transitional belts) was only 9-11 percent. It is highly probable that the mobility processes of the 1970s did not moderate this separation: the dwellings of the outer ring of housing estates became the 'depositaries' of social groups of the lower middle classes, while the dwellings in the green belts of the city were occupied by the upper classes.

This interpretation, along with P.A. Compton's suggestion of increased segregation resulting from the 1971 housing reforms, (French and Hamilton, 1979, p. 481) has been questioned by Sillince (1985b, pp. 146-7). He presents figures on the break-down between 'physical' (manual) and 'non-physical' workers, in each of the 22 districts of Budapest, for 1960, 1970 and 1980. The variance in these ratios has gone down sequentially from 1960 to 1970 and 1980, as is shown in Table 5.6. His interpretation is that social class segregation has progressively fallen over the 20 years. While the reduced variance is to some extent a reflection of the overall drop in the ratio as the proportion of non-physical workers has increased, the trend towards reduced inequality is confirmed, if less dramatically, by the coefficient of variation (standard deviation divided by the mean) and by the ratio of maximum to minimum district values.

The rankings of districts on the ratio of physical to non-physical workers shows a high degree of consistency from year to year. In other words, the pattern of social differentiation has not changed much over two decades. Figure 5.2 shows a distinct spatial concentration of districts based on this fairly crude socio-economic distinction, very much the same in 1960 and 1980, with the more physical or working-class districts concentrated in the south and west while those with a higher proportion of non-physical workers are in the central and western parts of the city.

However, this level of spatial subdivision may be too broad to reflect local differentiation making for more of a patchwork than the clear zonal pattern suggested in Figure 5.2. Szelenyi (1987, p. 5) reports work of Hungarian scholars who question the existence of large-scale occupational segregation in contemporary Budapest. While they found that those on the top of the social

Table 5.6   Ratio of physical to non-physical active and retired workers in Budapest districts 1960-1980: summary data

	1960	1970	1980
City of Budapest	1.91	1.32	1.07
Maximum district ratio	4.15	2.53	1.86
Minimum district ratio	0.82	0.52	0.41
Maximum : minumum	5.06	4.87	4.54
Variance	1.01	0.39	0.19
Coefficient of variation	0.44	0.41	0.37

Source: calculated from Sillince (1985b, p. 146, Table 5); ratios in original rounded to 2 places of decimals

hierarchy are concentrated in certain geographically identifiable areas, they claim that the poor are not. Socially homogeneous spaces in Budapest are small, they say, composed of groups of adjacent flats or family houses: microcosms randomly distributed in the macrospace of the city.

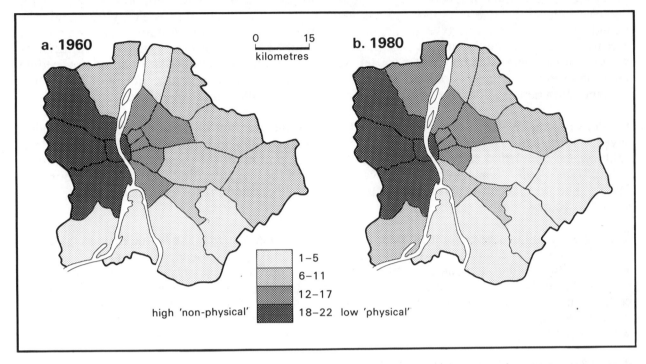

Figure 5.2 Districts of Budapest ranked according to the ratio of 'physical' to 'non-physical' workers, 1960 and 1980
Source: Table 5.6, data from Sillince (1985b, p. 146, Table 5)

Summary

This chapter has shown something of the complexity which can arise in the distribution of housing under socialism. Changing state policy has affected who gets what, where from housing, in both the state and private market sectors. It is tempting to see the continuing scale and significance of the private sector in Hungary as beneficial, yet the research reported here suggests that its role in the process of distribution is by no means egalitarian. As an integral part of the overall housing system, subject to varying degrees of state involvement, the private sector's contribution must be seen as a reflection of the structure of the society as a whole, rather than of some independent 'free market' element.

6. WARSAW: RE-CREATION OF SOCIALISM

It is the trade union Solidarity *(Solidarnosc)* rather than the state of Polish cities which has attracted most western attention in recent years. The two are by no means unrelated, however. A major concern behind the rise of Solidarity has been popular dissatisfaction with living standards, including what is perceived to be an increase in disparity between social groups. Far from being a call for a return to capitalism, as is sometimes assumed in the west, this major working-class movement has been asking socialism to 'deliver the goods', in the literal sense of supplying people with the living conditions associated with a modern industrial society in an efficient and equitable manner. Nowhere is the failure to do this more conspicuous than in urban Poland.

Poland's capital, Warsaw, occupies a special place in the creation of the socialist city. Founded seven centuries ago, it had become one of the six largest cities in Europe by the end of the 18th century. Its population had reached 600,000 by the beginning of the present century, and almost 1.3 million in 1939. Then five years of war devastated the city, leaving barely 162,000 people in 1945. The new society therefore had almost complete freedom to reconstruct a major city according to new ideals.

There is so much of interest in the modern re-creation of Warsaw that to confine discussion to our central theme of inequality is difficult. However, retaining this focus will enable us to place Warsaw within an unfolding analysis from which some common experience is emerging along with recognition of the distinctive nature of different socialist societies. A broader view of the city can be found in Grime and Weclawowicz (1981); background on urbanisation in Poland is reserved for the next chapter.

The development of modern Warsaw

A Polish publication on Warsaw (Arkady, 1981) provides the following brutal facts:

> Between 1939 and 1945 about 800 thousand people, or two-thirds of Warsaw's population, were killed. The city was 85 per cent devastated. Industry was 90 per cent destroyed, all bridges on the Vistula had been blown up, 80 per cent of all hospitals and clinics lay in rubble, educational institutions had been destroyed [by] 70 per cent, power grid - 50 per cent, gas mains - 70 per cent, water and sewage systems - 30 per cent, transport rolling stock - 87 per cent. Of the 987 historical monuments existing before 1939 the Nazis had completely destroyed 782. In January 1945 the city area was covered with a mass of rubble estimated at 20 million cubic metres.

Left-bank Warsaw, with the city centre, was practically non-existent, while on the right bank (east) of the River Vistula one building in four had been destroyed.

The first priority was to get the city working again, taking advantage of what remained of the productive capacity and infrastructure. This ensured that some elements of the pre-existing urban form would be preserved, whatever else might be the shape of the new Warsaw. High priority was also given to reconstruction of the historic core of the Stare Miasto or Old Town, along with rehabilitation of the surviving housing stock and construction of the first new apartment blocks. By 1949 sufficient progress had been made that idealism harnessed to practical necessity could be articulated as follows by the Polish President, Boleslaw Bierut (quoted in Regulska, 1987, p. 327):

> New Warsaw cannot be a reproduction of the old one, it cannot be only an improved repetition of prewar concentration of private capitalist interests of the society, it cannot be a reflection of contradictions dividing this society, it cannot be a scene and base for exploitation of people and expansion of privileges of the owners' class. ... New Warsaw should become the socialist capital. The fight for the ideological image of our city must be carried out with full consciousness and with all required energy directed towards this goal. New Warsaw through development of industry will become a centre of production, the city of workers.

It was a matter of principle that, under socialism, the state would attend to the housing needs of the population. This would have been a daunting task even without war damage, for Warsaw was one of the most overcrowded cities in Europe in the inter-war period. Physical reconstruction and industrialisation attracted large numbers of migrants to the city, which had 1 million people again by 1955. Restrictions on in-migration were introduced, and later a programme of industrial decentralisation to encourage more even regional development, but shortage of housing has continued to be one of the most serious problems facing Warsaw, and the country at large. As elsewhere in Eastern Europe, access to housing is thus a major source of differentiation, and inequality, in urban living.

Table 6.1 summarises the progress made in housing Warsaw's population since 1950. Not only have large numbers of dwellings been constructed, but there has also been a steady rise in standards measured by dwellings per household, inhabitants per room and floorspace per inhabitant. The improvement has not been perfectly regular over time, however; the largest average room size was achieved in the 1950s when some of the earliest state apartment blocks near the city centre were built to high standards (as in other socialist cities at the time). And the so-called 'crisis' of the 1980s has greatly reduced housing construction along with much other economic activity, so that in 1984 there were only half as many units built as in 1970.

Table 6.1 Housing the people of Warsaw 1950-1984

Numbers ('000s)	1950	1960	1970	1980	1984
Households	302	396	469	594	
Dwellings	199	308	408	535	566
Rooms	415	696	1036	1518	1633
Dwellings/household	0.66	0.78	0.87	0.87	
Inhabitants/room	1.98	1.64	1.27	1.05	1.01
Floorspace/inhabitant (sq. m.)			13.67	15.14	15.76

Source: Dangschat (1987, p. 41, Table 1); figures for households and dwellings per household 1980 based on 1978 census; gaps indicate no data available

In 1944 all existing housing was 'communalised' or taken into state ownership, except for small one-family dwellings. Most private housing remains on the outskirts of the city and of relatively poor quality, though some inner enclaves of single- or two-family villa-type homes of the pre-war middle class survive around the centre. New private construction is still permitted, accounting for about 7 percent of all housing and with an average size approaching twice that of communal provision. The advent of socialism saw the state (or city of Warsaw) take the major role in housing, but pressure on resources led to the encouragement of large-scale co-operative development from the late 1950s, tapping people's savings in return for a shorter waiting time. In the case of co-operatives for ownership as opposed to tenancy, where the down-payment is much larger, there are higher standards and the freedom to sell or leave to heirs (Ciechocinska, 1987, p. 11). The development of co-operatives was accompanied by a decline in city-financed construction, which was discontinued in 1973. Characteristics of the housing stock at the time of the 1978 census, just before the onset of the 'crisis', are summarised in Table 6.2.

Plate 15 (l) Early socialist-period flats in central Warsaw, built to relatively high standards. Plate 16 (r) New housing in the southern Warsaw district of Ursynow, remote from central services.

Table 6.2   **Characteristics of housing stock in Warsaw 1978**

Date of construction	%	Ownership	%	Number of rooms	%	Floor space (sq. m.)	%
Before 1918	3.8	State (city)	42.1	1-2	40.4	<30	17.5
1918-1944	19.1	Co-operative	40.4	3	32.3	30-49	51.6
1945-1970	54.6	Plants	7.7	4	22.1	50-79	26.1
1971-1978	22.5	Private	9.8	5>	5.2	80>	4.8
Total	100.0	Total	100.0	Total	100.0	Total	100.0

Source: Ciéchocinska (1987, p. 11, Table 1)

Relatively unconstrained by its pre-existing form, the overall structure of the city could develop according to the prevailing socialist planning practice, influenced by Soviet experience. Figure 6.1 shows the city of 1990 as planned. The 1980s saw setbacks in all kinds of construction, but this map broadly indicates how Warsaw is today. Land use is differentiated largely by wedges, extended beyond the city limits along major transport lines.

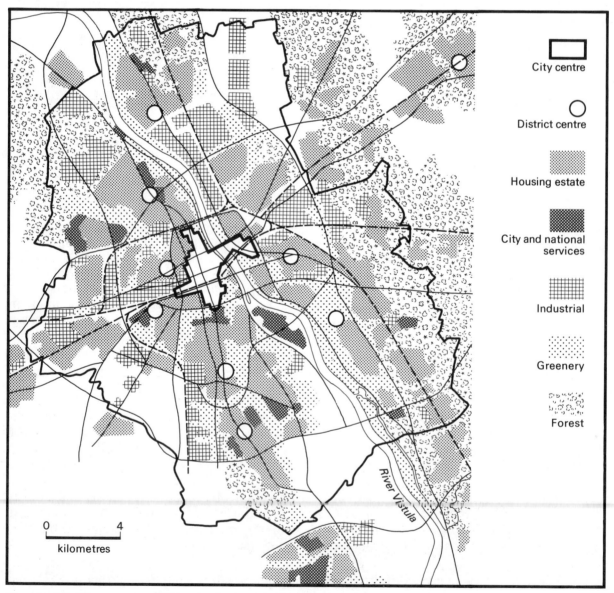

Figure 6.1 Warsaw in 1990, as planned at the beginning of the 1980s
Source: Arkady (1981)

The central quarters of districts form part of a hierarchical spatial structure of service provision. The *microraion* or neighbourhood unit concept was adopted, having had some antecedents in pre-war Warsaw in the form of 'community estates' set up to improve the lives of the poor (Malicka, 1979, pp. 211-12). Figure 6.2 illustrates the layout of a modern housing estate in the southern part of the city, with local services along with apartment blocks. However, there is uneven development of the service infrastructure, as in the Soviet city, with central areas tending to fare better. In the initial period co-operatives paid much more attention than municipal authorities to the appearance of housing estates and supply of services, but as co-operatives came to dominate the scene such concerns seem to have been less important (Ciechocinska, 1987, p. 11). Modern estates on the fringe of the city may lack good transport as well as services, though quality of accommodation may be some compensation. Thus urban environmental attributes as well as the dwellings themselves will vary with location, date of construction and housing tenure.

Plate 17 (l) Varied design and landscaping characterises the more attractive residential areas in the Natolin development in Warsaw's southern district of Ursynow (see Figure 6.2 for layout of this neighbourhood). Plate 18 (r) Superior block of flats near the centre of Warsaw, built by a co-operative for members of the architectural profession.

The socio-economic spatial structure of Warsaw 1931 and 1970

In Chapter 3 we were able to see something of the impact of the socialist period on Prague, which retained much of its pre-war urban fabric. A similar exercise is possible for Warsaw, but in quite different conditions associated with the almost total re-creation of the city under socialism. The source is a monograph by Weclawowicz (1975), the results of which are most accessible in French and Hamilton (1979, pp. 387-423). The technique is the same as used in Prague, and need not be explained here; suffice it to say that it extracts composite indicators from data on a large number of variables, which can then be mapped to reveal patterns of variation to which many different conditions contribute.

In 1931 Warsaw had a population of 1,171,900. The major influences on the city's spatial structure were industrialisation under capitalism and consequent changes in socio-occupational structure of the population, along with the functions of capital of Poland. The city was both growing and changing rapidly. Weclawowicz assembled data for enumeration districts, on 26 variables measuring population characteristics, occupation and housing. From these he derived an index accounting for more than half the variance in the original set of data, which he labelled *economic-class position*. It was very much a reflection of occupational status and housing conditions. A second but less important dimension of variation strongly reflected the distribution of the large Jewish population which, although spatially concentrated, was subject to the same economic forces and internal differentiation as the rest of the population.

Figure 6.3a and b show elements of the socio-economic spatial structure of Warsaw in 1931. The distribution of the working-class population was closely association with housing quality measured by availability of piped water and sanitation; the higher proportion of workers in a district, the

50

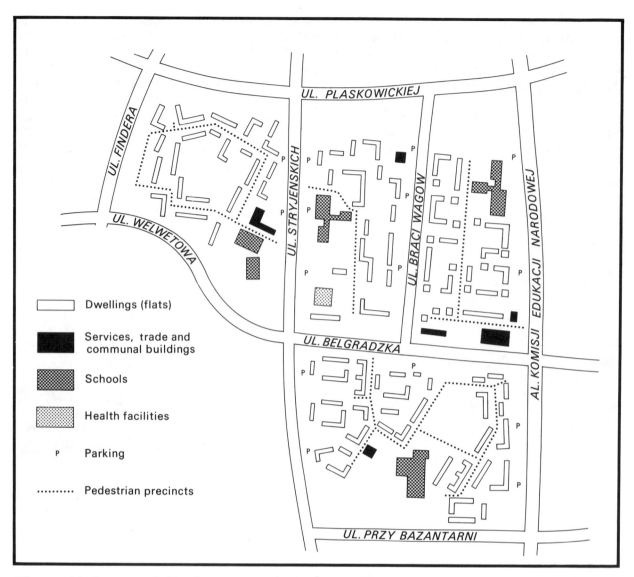

Figure 6.2 Layout of housing estate of the late 1970s at Wyzyny in the Ursynow-Natolin district on the southern edge of Warsaw
Source: redrawn from plan on public display

Legend:
- Dwellings (flats)
- Services, trade and communal buildings
- Schools
- Health facilities
- P Parking
- .... Pedestrian precincts

poorer the housing. Figure 6.3c maps the distribution of the Jewish population, most intense in the ghetto on the northern edge of the city centre. Figure 6.3d provides a summary, in which district scores on the index of economic-class position have superimposed on them the Jewish ghetto as the city's major area of ethnic differentiation.

Weclawowicz recognised a pattern of concentric zones, with some elements of sectoral development. There was a clear decline in socio-economic status, from the compact central zone, through a continuous transitional zone, and out into a peripheral zone. This reversal of the usual generalisation concerning the capitalist city could be explained by the fact that the process of outward movement of wealthier people had begun in Warsaw only after 1918, generating few high-status areas on the periphery. Nevertheless, the population was sharply differentiated by class and ethnic group, which expressed itself in marked spatial differentiation.

The population of Warsaw in 1970, at 1,315,000, was not very much greater than in 1931. But the physical structure of the city had been very largely renewed, and the population itself had grown much more by selective in-migration (800,000 since 1945) reflecting the demands of the economy, than by natural increase in situ (190,000). Weclawowicz chose 40 variables which could only partially coincide with those available in 1931, to measure population characteristics, social status, occupation, education and housing attributes. Data were compiled for over 900 districts, thus giving a much finer spatial disaggregation than before.

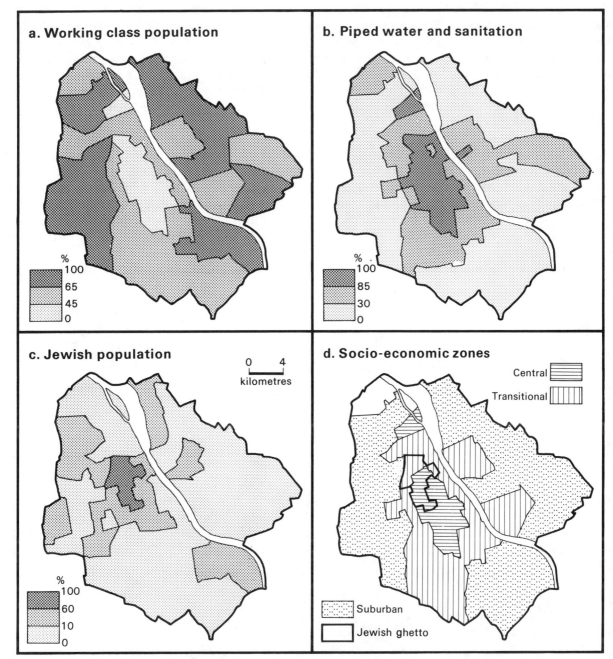

Figure 6.3 Features of socio-economic space in Warsaw 1931
Source: Weclawowicz (1975, pp. 48, 49, 52 and 61, Figs 9, 10, 12 and 19)

Plate 19 (l) *Highly valued villa-style housing built in the inter-war years for the bourgeoisie, in the Zoliborz district of Warsaw.* *Plate 20* (r) *Enclave of superior private housing close to the Old Town in central Warsaw, with the Mercedes car suggesting that privileges here are not confined to housing.*

About 30 percent of the variance in these data sets could be accounted for by an index reflecting certain educational and occupational characteristics along with form of housing tenure.   This captured what Weclawowicz termed *socio-occupational position*, rather than economic-class status as in 1931, because it was less concerned with the income differentials which predominate under capitalism than with the broader social evaluation of labour in particular occupations. In other words, the state rather than the market had become the means of assigning relative significance to different occupations.

District scores on this index are mapped in Figure 6.4. The highest tend to be in the central part of the city, reflecting the concentration of writers, journalists and artists, etc. along with others occupying crucial (and privileged) positions and working in nearby offices, educational institutions and so on. This was the outcome of a selective housing policy which enabled these groups to settle in central locations which had been rebuilt soon after the war. The lowest scores denote areas dominated by housing construction of the 1960s when co-operatives were coming to the fore. They comprise large islands, separated by outliers of higher scores.

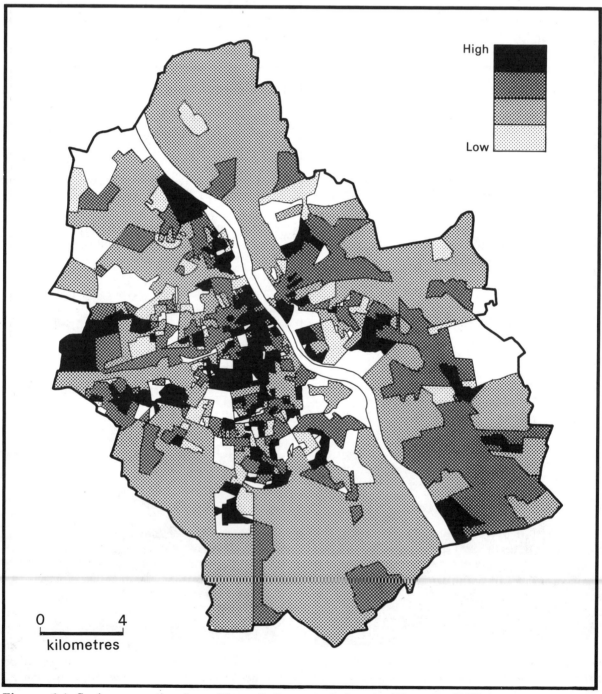

Figure 6.4 Socio-occupational position of the population in Warsaw 1970
Source: Weclawowicz (1975, p. 90, Fig. 30)

Weclawowicz concluded that there were great differences in spatial structure between 1931 and 1970. In the inter-war period Warsaw had an urban form typical of capitalism, strongly differentiated by both class and ethnicity (Polish/Jewish). The pattern in 1970 was more a reflection of socio-occupational position, a selective housing policy, and stages of settling the post-war city. The classic models, with their wedges, concentric zones and multiple-nuclear patterns, are too simplistic to describe the reality of the city's spatial structure. The Warsaw of 1970 was more of a mosaic, differentiated in local detail. This may have reflected a city still in transition, with some influence of an old form on which the new was being imposed.

Socio-spatial disparities in contemporary Warsaw

The nearest we can get to an up-to-date picture of socio-spatial disparities in Warsaw is the end of the 1970s. The crisis-ridden 1980s have been peculiar years, data on this period are limited, and the later 1970s probably represent the post-war city at the height of its achievements to date, at least with respect to housing conditions and general living standards.

Data from the National Census of 1978 have been used by Dangschat and Blasius (1987; see also Dangschat, 1987), to develop a typology of Warsaw's planning districts. Their 22 variables measure mainly education levels and age of the population along with age of housing stock, construction agency and utilities. Adopting a similar method to Weclawowicz, they identify four distinct clusters of districts defined mainly on the basis of housing age and type. These are:

I   Districts with a high proportion of privately owned dwellings around the city's periphery. These districts are relatively sparsely populated and dominated by agriculture or industry. Much of the housing stock will be of rural-type construction.

II   Districts marked by a high proportion of dwellings built before 1918 or between 1945 and 1970, predominantly state owned, and with the age group 50-64 heavily represented in the population. These are mainly in or near the city centre. This is the area in which housing reconstruction started after the war, young families coming in and tending to remain because of restricted intra-urban mobility - hence the age structure. Also included are some old districts of poor housing in Praga on the right bank.

III   Districts in which the upper educational groups and age group 40-49 are heavily represented, and forming a circle around the city centre. They include some quarters with mainly private single- or two-family houses built between the wars for the bourgeoisie, as well as housing estates of the 1960s.

IV   Districts with a high proportion of co-operatives built during the 1970s, households of 3-4 persons, and 30-39-year-olds. This cluster shows a sectoral pattern within a discontinuous ring around cluster III.

Figure 6.5a shows a distinct pattern of these clusters, tending towards concentric zones but with wedges interrupting the outer cluster I. Figure 6.5b highlights some of the more distinctive districts in and around the central part of the city, where marked contrasts in housing can be observed. In so far as these differences represent the spatial sorting of different kinds of people, socio-spatial disparities can be recognised.

Education appears to be an important means whereby access to a differentiated housing stock is determined. Dangschat (1987, p. 46) maps the population of Warsaw by four different measures of educational attainment, showing distinct concentrations in different parts of the city. The association between education and housing is summarised as follows (Dangschat and Blasius, 1987, pp. 188-9):

Better educated people live in new, well-equipped co-operative dwellings; the poorly educated live either mainly in single-person households in very old houses, badly equipped in the inner city parts of Praga ... or as bigger families in the rural outskirts in private small houses which are badly equipped. These concentrations are spatially adjacent. Their spatial position can best be described by a model of concentric circles, which are overlapped by sectoral patterns in the outer districts.

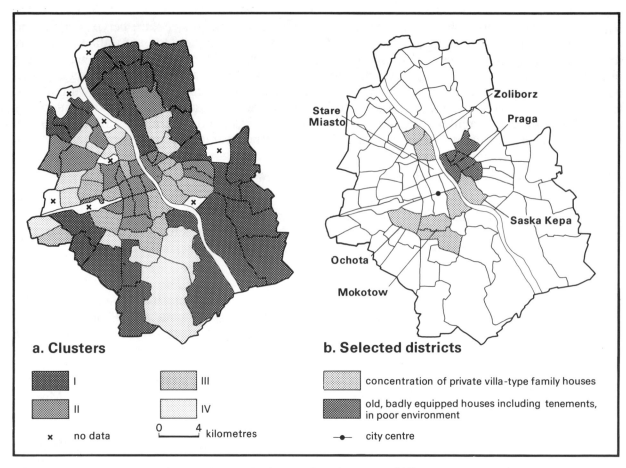

Figure 6.5 Socio-spatial differentiation of Warsaw 1978 based mainly on housing characteristics
Source: a. Dangschat and Blasius (1987, p. 181. Fig 4); b. indications in Dangschat and Blasius (1987)

Too much should not be made of these stark distinctions, however. There is also the concentration of well educated in the inner city, in nice single-family villas as well as good apartments, and people of low educational level living in old and badly equipped houses in these same areas, leading to nearby neighbourhoods of the highest and lowest educational groups (Dangschat, 1987, p. 43).

If education along with associated occupational position significantly differentiates access to housing, it is the varying character of housing stock patterned by Warsaw's post-war development that gives social disparities their spatial expression. This is summarised by Dangschat and Blasius (1987, p. 189) as follows:

> The rapid reconstruction led to a ring-like expansion of the city. The heavily destroyed inner city areas had been rebuilt during the late 1940s and early 1950s partly with supra-standard apartments. Only the inner areas of Praga on the right bank of the river Vistula survived the damage; that housing now represents the worst conditions in the city. In the north ... and the south of the downtown ... some two-storey double- or row-houses are left and kept occupied by former bourgeois families. The rest of that area up to the former boundaries of the city was rebuilt during the late 1950s and the 1960s. This area is followed by a ring of multi-storey co-operative dwellings. The periphery is characterised by relatively low population density in many areas, where part of the housing stock dates back to the time before their incorporation of 1951 within the city.

These authors agree with Szelenyi (1983) that housing inequalities do not counteract other inequalities but tend to reinforce them. They claim that disparities in Warsaw, as a 'socialist' city, are not fundamentally different in a descriptive sense from those of their West European counterparts.

An alternative position is advanced by Ciechocinska (1987, pp. 22-4), who is closer to Weclawowicz in asserting that 'The pattern of sociospatial differences in Warsaw differs considerably from text-book examples of social inequalities which occur in many developed and third world countries'. She sees the basic source of inequality as the shortage of housing, which generates a distinctive process of differential access. The shortage can mean a wait of well over 10 years in a housing co-operative, but especially valuable employees such as those in managerial or leadership positions in public organisations have a better chance of obtaining such flats. Only families with incomes well below average can obtain city-owned flats, and their concentration usually in older parts leads to strong socio-spatial differentiation. Very affluent people can buy an owner-type flat or build a one-family house, but the cost is extremely high: she cites a typical flat for a family of three in Warsaw at the equivalent of more than 20 years' average pay.

Another differentiating factor is the time when a new flat was obtained. Changing standards of provision mean that there are whole estates where average living space per person is lower than in other areas, as is development of the service network. Land availability means that new projects increasingly tend to be on the outskirts, where transport and infrastructure lag behind and more time has to be spent on commuting.

Rigid regulations concerning the exchange of flats, along with the housing shortage, means that most people are tied to their accommodation virtually for life. Such stability is conducive to a perpetuation of the existing differences in the socio-spatial structure of towns. This includes demographic differences between individual housing estates, as people pass through stages of the life cycle in situ rather than moving with changing individual or family needs.

Ciechocinska (1987, p. 24) concludes her argument as follows:

The factors enumerated above lead to the emergence of large population-space differences in urban areas. They form complex patterns of spatial configurations. It would be deceptive to employ the notion of social segregation used by western urban sociologists for this process. These sociospatial differences are determined to a much greater degree by the factor noted above than by social and professional status or education. The problem of ethnic minorities does not exist in Warsaw, so there is no tendency to form enclaves inhabited by individual ethnic groups; neither is there a problem of gastarbeiters [migrant workers] or the unemployed.

Thus there are distinctive patterns and processes in socio-spatial disparities within the Polish version of the socialist city.

Social disorder: the case of crime

There are allusions in the literature to the spatial congregation of people with various manifestations of social disorder or pathology. For example, Dangschat (1987, p. 51) cites Polish research which found spatial concentrations of 'social dropouts', including adolescent and juvenile criminals, persons supported by public funds, alcoholics and homicides. Firm facts on conditions usually attributed to the evils of capitalism are hard to find for any socialist city. However, there is some limited information on crime in Warsaw which is worth reviewing briefly.

That crime rates at the broad district level within Warsaw may have been related to local environmental (housing) conditions in the 1960s is shown in Table 6.3. By far the highest level of criminal activity was in Praga Polnoc, which had the lowest proportion of flats with the various facilities indicated. This district also had the highest birth rate, death rate, and proportion of rural migrants. The districts with the lowest crime rates (Mokotow and Zoliborz) had markedly better housing than Praga. The best housing conditions were in the central Srodmiescie district, but the crime rate here was second highest on the west bank. By 1970/71 this district had the highest crime rate in the city (see Figure 6.6a), reflecting the development of the modern city centre and its increased opportunities for theft.

Areas the size of Warsaw's seven districts can hide considerable variations, of course, and more detail may be required for adequate interpretation. A hint of what can be revealed at a finer spatial scale is provided by figures for burglary by census tracts shown in Figure 6.6b. Warsaw had

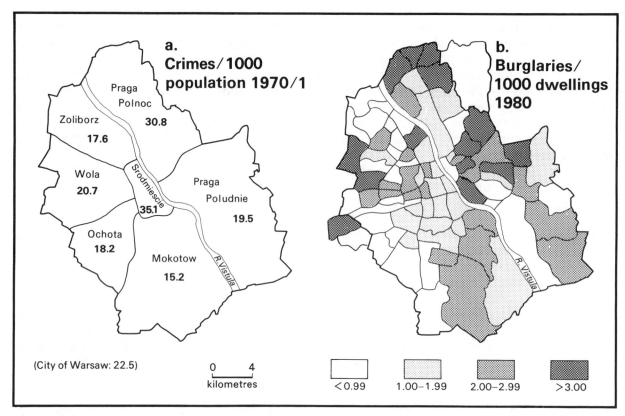

Figure 6.6 The geography of crime in Warsaw 1970/1 and 1980
Sources: a. data from French and Hamilton (1979, p. 281, Table 10.2); b. Bartnicki (1986, p. 240, Fig. 2)

Table 6.3   The relationship between crime and housing conditions in Warsaw districts 1960/1

District	Crime rate per 10,000 popn	% of flats with:			
		running water	sewerage	gas	central heating
Srodmiescie	146	94	93	79	64
Mokotow	118	80	80	70	60
Ochota	128	68	69	45	43
Wola	158	82	80	55	44
Zoliborz	124	80	80	69	57
Praga Polnoc	220	64	60	30	16
Praga Poludnie	148	63	65	32	27
City of Warsaw	150	75	75	53	43

Source: French and Hamilton (1979, p. 281, Table 10.2); percentages from original rounded

almost 14 percent of Poland's recorded burglaries in 1980, and over 19 percent in 1984. Bartnicki (1986, pp. 240-1) points to the difference between the pattern in Warsaw and that in the American city with its concentration in the centre and diminishing incidence towards the periphery. In Warsaw the areas of relatively high crime risk are the housing estates of the 1970s. This is associated with demographic and family structure, lack of technical infrastructure, size of the estates, and the ease with which burglary can be committed and not noticed by neighbours.

While northern and western peripheral areas stand out in Figure 6.6b, so does Praga on the east bank. This district remains notorious for its crime, and general social and environmental degradation. Its ambience is well captured by the journalist Roger Boyes (**The Times**, 12 May 1986):

The undressed buildings of Praga, pale and pockmarked by war, house the highest concentration of criminals in Warsaw. It is not Brixton or the Bronx, but it is tough. At dusk, a half-gloom settles on the long courtyards. The fuses and bulbs have been looted from the street lamps, and people lurch rather than walk, giving the impression that the whole district has been etherized. This is not far from the truth; in Praga over the past year all murderers, rapists and car thieves, 70 per cent of those involved in brawls, and 65 per cent of muggers were under the influence of alcohol when they committed their crimes. And 95 per cent of the victims were drunk. ... The criminal epicentre of Praga is the Bazaar Rozyckiego, an open-air market in which, like a crooked Harrods, one can buy anything. Hot goods find their fences here, foreign currencies find their customers, tarts find their pimps. The ripples spread outwards, engulfing two suburban railway stations that carry thousands of villagers in and out of Warsaw every day - easy pickings, most of them, after a couple of drinks.

Some Poles who know London see Praga as Warsaw's East End, or at least an evocation of the old working-class quarters of the capitalist city, which socialism was supposed to eliminate.

*Plate 21 (l) The Praga district of Warsaw, preserving something of the ambience of pre-war working-class areas and known for high levels of social pathology such as crime. **Plate 22** (r) The Kazimierz district of Cracow, a former Jewish ghetto which escaped wartime destruction, now characterised by decaying urban fabric and a relatively poor population.*

Objective and subjective evaluations of residential space

Different parts of a city will be viewed in different ways by different people, according to their attitudes and needs, as we found in Moscow. In Warsaw even Praga has its attractions, for those seeking scarce goods and services. But how far do the subjective evaluations of the people of Warsaw correspond with a more objective assessment of different parts of the city?

Some evidence is provided by Swianiewicz (1986). He analysed the subjective attractiveness of districts based on newspaper advertisements for free-market apartments. A 50 percent variation in the price was observed, apartments in the centre being most expensive but with almost as high prices in the inner quarters of Mokotow and Zoliborz and in Saska Kepa on the right bank (all areas with pre-war villas). Figure 6.7a shows the varying levels of attraction assigned to different parts of the city. New housing districts on the outskirts have the lowest evaluation, owing to commuting difficulties, shortage of services and the quality of prefabricated apartments.

A more objective evaluation was undertaken on the basis of 26 measures of housing, environment, transportation, and accessibility to services. The results are shown in Figure 6.7b, as 'attractive' and 'problem' areas. The four problem areas are as follows:

1. North-western, with poor access to services and transportation, poor housing in the majority of districts and also local environmental problems.

2. South-eastern, with a common problem of availability of services, and in some districts also of housing conditions.

58

3. West-centre, with very poor environmental conditions and very high congestion.

4. Right-bank, with a very low value of measures representing all elements of living standards.

The attractive areas were defined on the basis of having no more than two variables below what were regarded as critical values.

Comparison between the subjective and objective evaluations show some similarities. For example both identify inner Mokotow and Zoliborz, part of Ochta, and the Old Town. The differences are most marked with respect to parts of the inner city, where people seem prepared to recognise better housing conditions along with accessibility to transport and services as a major source of attraction, assigning less importance to the congestion, noise and pollution which make these central areas less attractive objectively. This presumably reflects a hierarchy of values: the general housing problem and poverty of social and technical infrastructure leave people with less regard for some other environmental conditions.

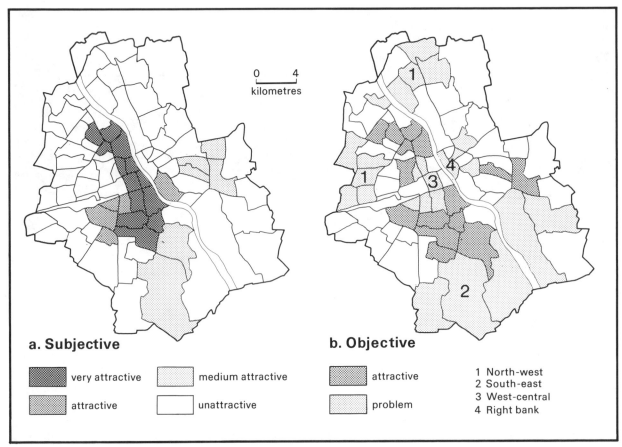

Figure 6.7 Subjective and objective evaluations of the attractiveness of urban terrain in Warsaw c.1980
Source: Swianiewicz (1986, pp. 235 and 237, Figs 2 and 3)

Summary

While the Warsaw of 1945 may not have provided the socialist planners with a perfectly clean slate, most of what the war had left invited erasure. However, a differentiated housing stock has developed, much less from the survival of remnants of the pre-war city and reconstruction of its historic core than from city planning and construction practice itself. People with high occupational status or working for powerful employers are advantaged in access to good housing in attractive locations, along with associated services and environmental quality. While social criteria may assist access to housing of moderate quality, the privileged treatment of others under conditions of continuing shortage places the needy at a disadvantage - the more so as co-operatives requiring personal investment have come to dominate 'communal' provision. The outcome is a distinctive pattern and process of inequality.

7. URBAN INEQUALITY IN POLAND: EVIDENCE FROM OTHER CITIES

How far is the experience of Warsaw typical of the Polish city under socialism? Warsaw does have unique features, arising from its size, status as capital, and economic significance, as well as from the extent of war damage and the importance attached to restoration of its historic and architectural heritage. But some other cities have experienced rapid development associated with industrialisation, along with reconstruction of a devastated 'old town'. And a similar spatial form could be expected throughout the urban system of a nation explicitly directed towards centrally determined objectives. In this chapter we shall see what other cities can reveal of the Polish experience of inequality under socialism. But first some background on urbanisation more generally.

Urbanisation in Poland

Before the Second World War, Poland was one of the least urbanised countries in Europe. The subsequent growth of the urban population has been rapid, from about 37 percent of the total in 1950 to over 60 percent at the end of the 1980s. With a qualifying size of 5000 inhabitants, there were over 800 towns and cities in Poland in 1986, with a combined population of 22.7 million. Table 7.1 shows the numbers and populations in the largest size categories, and how they have grown since 1970.

Table 7.1 Numbers and populations ('000s) of larger cities in Poland 1970-1986

Population size	1970		1980		1986	
	no.	popn	no.	popn	no.	popn
50,000 - 99,999	27	1871	38	2614	45	3097
100,000-199,999	14	2193	22	3090	22	3028
200,000 and over	10	5195	15	7347	18	8293

Source: **Rocznik Demograficzny 1987** (Demographic Yearbook of Poland), Warsaw 1988

Table 7.2 Population ('000s) of Poland's ten largest cities 1950-1986

City	1950	1960	1970	1980	1986
Warsaw	804	1139	1316	1596	1665
Bydgoszcz	163	232	282	359	396
Gdansk	195	287	366	457	468
Katowice	225	270	305	355	367
Cracow	344	481	590	716	744
Lublin	117	181	239	304	330
Lodz	620	710	763	836	847
Poznan	321	408	472	553	578
Szczecin	179	269	338	388	395
Wroclaw	309	431	526	618	640

Source: **Rocznik Demograficzny 1987**

Table 7.2 shows the growth of Poland's ten largest cities, all of which have one-third of a million or more people today. Like Warsaw, many of them have more than doubled their population since 1950.

Planning for urban equality

Polish cities varied in the extent to which wartime destruction provided a need for rapid reconstruction, and with it the opportunity to create a new spatial structure. Urban development was closely associated with industrialisation and major population movements, as people who had been displaced returned to the cities and large numbers of migrants from the countryside came in looking for the work which agriculture could no longer provide.

From the outset, urban planning had both practical and ideological objectives. Nowakowski (1979, p. 205) summarises this as follows:

> By stimulating industrialization and urbanization, the Polish authorities aimed to provide people with satisfactory dwelling conditions, thus making their adaptation to new conditions and a new environment easier. Also, they aimed to form an egalitarian society, having equally well-equipped housing estates in the new towns where all social categories could share similar conditions, thus enabling the immigrant peasants to achieve a higher socio-cultural and economic level. Housing estates, especially the cooperative ones, were regarded as the main focus of this social policy. This was where the peasant arriving in a town would become integrated into the new community and take advantage of the socio-cultural facilities and institutions.

The process of integration and socialisation was crucial to the development of the new society, for people from the countryside tend to be conservative rather than in the vanguard of the revolution. The authorities wanted workers with the right attitudes, and saw the form and facilities of the cities as a means to this end.

This egalitarian orientation in Polish urban development was not entirely new, however. Pre-war experiments with co-operative estates, as in Warsaw, meant that there were precedents for the adoption of neighbourhood planning with attention to services as well as housing provision. Two important precepts in Polish spatial planning are 'the right to adequate living conditions in cities - by the proper location of service centres for education, culture, etc.' and 'the principle of social equality - by applying uniform criteria with respect to every social group and area' (Regulska, 1987, p. 326). That ideals were not easily translated into reality can be attributed to both organisational and behavioural factors.

Organisational problems have arisen from the failure to integrate planning - central and local, economic and social. For a long time after the war the priority given to industrial growth at the national level restricted the expenditure required to achieve social objectives in the cities. Initially the more effective planning was confined to large cities with massive reconstruction problems, and it was 1972 before effective integration of economic and physical planning was achieved along with more devolution of decisions concerning local provision of housing, social services and infrastructure. 'Poorly functioning cities in turn restricted the efficiency of the national economy. This spiral generated a gap between the quality of urban life and popular demands' (Regulska, 1987, p. 335). And from this stems the current 'crisis', and challenge to the authorities by a frustrated working class.

At the behavioural level, attempts to use urban form to create new social attitudes can be frustrated by the population itself, in a state where every human action cannot be planned for and controlled. Social equality is supposed to be encouraged by residential heterogeneity, i.e. families in varied occupations living side by side. Sieminski (1979) reviews research on the city of Lublin which claimed to have found heterogeneous settlements both integrated and egalitarian, with close relationships between families of different socio-occupational affiliations on their common staircase, although there was more selective interaction in other parts of the building or settlement. He is sceptical about the egalitarian interpretation, pointing out that, even if there is interaction, the mix of manual and white-collar workers will lead to differences in ways of life which are bound to form a basis for association among people. Furthermore, there is a constant process of spatial selectivity in the larger cities: 'the character of many settlements and small districts, which were originally socially diversified, became, in the course of time, ever more homogeneous with a decided predominance of either workers, clerks or intelligentsia' (Sieminski, 1979, p. 225).

The greatest likelihood of finding something approaching socio-spatial equality would appear to be in the specialised industrial towns or cities which were an important feature of the early phase of socialism. These were usually built on virgin sites, to support a plant large enough to generate major economies of scale. The archetypal case in Poland is Nowa Huta, which adjoins the city of Cracow. Construction of the Lenin steel works was begun here in 1949. By the early 1980s employment had risen to 35,000, and the population of Nowa Huta to roughly 250,000. It is difficult to do more than speculate on how egalitarian a city Nowa Huta might be. The dominance of one industry as a source of employment makes for occupational homogeneity, but there must be some workers with crucial technical or managerial skills which may be a source of privilege. Much of the population came from a similar rural background (in 1970, three-quarters were described as of peasant origin), which suggests similarity of attitudes and life styles. The residential areas reveal varied building styles and layouts, as in other cities, reflecting period of construction (see Pounds, Dziewonski, Kortus and Vlassenbroeck, 1981, pp. 20-25), but this is not to say that there are corresponding differences in status and living standards.

Overall, Nowa Huta is not regarded as a major success for socialist planning. The steel works may perform its allotted role in the national economy, but as a place to live Nowa Huta has a distinctively industrial ambience exacerbated by air pollution and the erosion of open space for urban expansion. But there is another more profound reason for questioning the project's success. There was a political motive in setting up a large industrial settlement in this particular location near Cracow: to bring the influence of a new socialist working class to bear on an old conservative city. It is one of the great ironies of Polish planning that Nowa Huta in fact became second only to Gdansk as a bastion of the trade union Solidarity, motivated by socialist ideals but challenging the Communist Party rather than the staid burgers of Cracow.

The intra-urban structure of Polish cities

Until the 1970s research on the intra-urban structure of Polish cities tended to avoid the issue of social inequality. The first major work on socio-spatial structure was that of Weclawowicz on Warsaw (reviewed in the previous chapter) and A. Jagielski on Wroclaw. The findings in Wroclaw identified competition between different social groups for better locations; as in Warsaw, the main differentiating factor was occupation and its impact on housing allocation. Jagielski (1986) has mapped the ratio of non-manual workers to manual workers in Wroclaw (typically about 1.0), to reveal distinct clusters of the non-manuals. Figure 7.1 shows that this pattern is closely associated with that of population having high-school education. There are high status wedges running outwards from around the city centre, penetrating the predominantly working-class outer estates. The western cluster tends to be of pre-war villas occupied by professionals, while the southern wedge is the preferred area of state housing for these groups.

Weclawowicz (1981) has attempted to find out how far the results obtained in Warsaw and Wroclaw are more broadly representative. He chose the nine cities of Lodz, Cracow, Lublin, Czestochowa, Radom, Olsztyn, Rzeszow, Opole and Slupsk, and performed the same analysis as he had in Warsaw. From data on 40 measures of population characteristics, occupation, education, family structure and housing in 1970, he identified socio-occupational position as the main component of variation in all but one of the cities, just as in Warsaw.

Each city was found to have its own pattern, though with some similarities. For example, Radom had the clearest distinction between an integrated area of highest socio-occupational position surrounded by lower scores, Czestochowa had a similar pattern but with some dispersal of high areas, while Cracow had high areas concentrated in sectors to the west and east of the Old Town. Two of the cities are illustrated in Figure 7.2, with only the highest and lowest areas identified to throw the patterns into relief. In Lublin the majority of areas with highest scores were in a sector to the west of the centre, the centre itself having rather a mosaic pattern, while the lowest areas were in blocks around the fringe. In Lodz, the highest scores were concentrated in the centre but with some scatter outwards; the lowest areas tended to be on the fringe but, again, with some scattering. Such differences as these reflect the way in which the cities are subdivided for statistical purposes, as well as their distinctive histories and processes of residential growth.

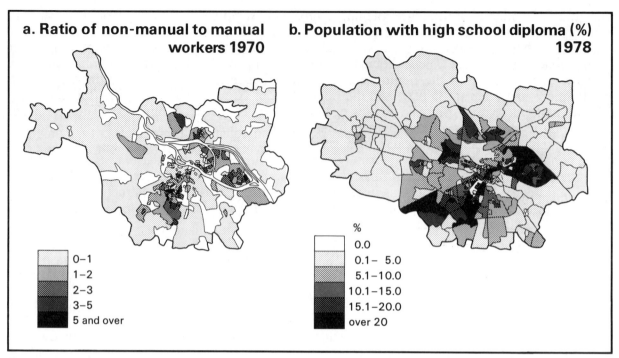

Figure 7.1 Ratio of non-manual to manual workers 1970 and population with high school education 1978 in Wroclaw
Source: Jagielski (1986, pp. 149-50, Figs 2 and 3)

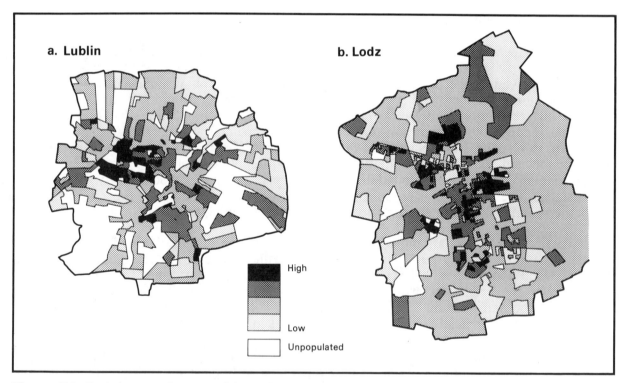

Figure 7.2 Socio-occupational position of the population in Lublin and Lodz 1970
Source: Weclawowicz (1981, pp. 191 and 193, Figs 4 and 6)

Weclawowicz emphasised the mosaic character of these cities, as he had in Warsaw. It seemed that we were witnessing the formation of a new intra-urban pattern, probably typical of the future socialist city. Again, the main differentiating processes are to be found in housing policies reflecting the social value of labour, and in family structure.

The socio-spatial structure of Radom 1970-1978

In a subsequent study, Weclawowicz (1985) has examined changes in the city of Radom between 1970 and the 1978 census. Radom had been particularly neglected in terms of expenditure on housing; research in the late 1970s had shown conditions there to be the worst among Polish cities with over 100,000 people. 'The inhabitants of new housing estates were provided with fairly homogeneous but relatively good housing. However, there still remained that part of the population who lived in large areas characterized by bad housing. The chances of leaving such areas was greater for higher socio-occupational groups (Weclawowicz, 1985, p. 86).

Between 1970 and 1978, 12,500 dwellings were built in Radom, accounting for a quarter of the city's total at the end of this period. But rapid population growth (from 160,000 to 186,000) meant that the housing shortage actually grew. And many people still lived in small and over-populated dwellings without basic facilities: over 31 percent of households shared their flat, only 59 percent had central heating and 72 percent water closets. New construction did not necessarily solve housing problems, however; a survey of people who received new apartments showed that 35 percent described them as too small and 25 percent regarded the standard of technical equipment as too low. Weclawowicz (1985, pp. 86-7) suspected that 'it was not an accident that Radom - that pole of urban poverty - became one of the main centres of political struggle in the 1970s and early 1980s'.

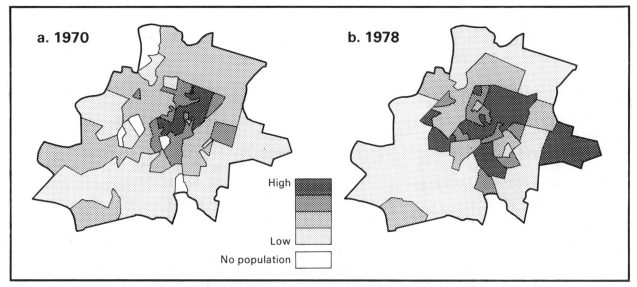

Figure 7.3 Socio-occupational position of the population of Radom 1970 and 1978
Source: Weclawowicz (1985, p. 90, Figs 1 and 2)

Weclawowicz was concerned about whether the changes in Radom during the 1970s had affected the whole city and its population, or only some social groups. He repeated the kind of analysis undertaken earlier, using 31 identical measures of occupation, education and housing for 1970 and 1978. The now-familiar socio-occupational position emerged as the leading component of internal variation in both years. The spatial pattern had changed somewhat, as Figure 7.3 shows (although this reflected different internal subdivisions for the two years as well as the impact of major housing developments). The general interpretation, based on detailed statistical analysis, was that an increase in spatial segregation had been brought about by the greater separation of elderly people in small households inhabiting old buildings from younger and larger households in more modern dwellings of higher standard. The gain from new development had therefore been unequally distributed. Weclawowicz (1985, p. 96) elaborated as follows:

New dwellings grouped in housing estates were an object of rivalry between different groups of population. Better access to new housing of good standard is given to the part of the population representing professions which are higher in the social hierarchy or economically and politically stronger. It should be pointed out, however, that not everyone competed for these new dwellings, as housing needs of a part of the population were already met.

The higher occupational groups had been better off in terms of housing in 1970. Some indication of which groups improved their position is provided by population composition of the estates built in 1971-78. In 1978, 23.7 percent of specialists and middle professional staff, 21.5 percent of clerks, 23.5 percent of physicians, 24.2 percent of research workers, and 26.9 percent of the writers, journalists, artists and actors lived on these estates, compared with 16.8 percent of all manual workers in the city. Workers dominated the new estates in absolute numbers, but they had improved their conditions to the smallest extent in relation to other occupational groups.

Social differentiation in the inner city

So far, we have been concerned with fairly broad patterns of intra-city inequality. To conclude with a taste of more local detail, a study by Prawelska-Skrzypek (1988) enables us to focus on the experience of some central city neighbourhoods. The author's aim was to show that, after the post-war mixing of population, a process of gradual segregation has been taking place, resulting in marked inter-neighbourhood differentiation within Polish cities. Old central city neighbourhoods are usually differentiated by both social structure and physical environment.

One area in each of the south-eastern Polish cities of Jaroslaw, Krosno, Nowy Sacz, Rzeszow and Tarnow was chosen, along with two in Cracow (Kazimierz and Srodmiescie). Before the war most central areas were inhabited by poor people, largely Jews, though the Srodmiescie district of Cracow was an elite neighbourhood. Cracow's Kazimierz was an exception to the Nazi custom of destroying the ghetto when the inhabitants had been shipped off to concentration camps; it was subsequently reoccupied by non-Jews, but still retains some landscape features of the Jewish ghettos which have otherwise disappeared from the Polish urban scene.

Affluent people have usually shown little interest in flats in old central city neighbourhoods, because of the poor condition of buildings and local infrastructure. Planned reconstruction and modernisation has often been prevented by lack of resources. In the neighbourhoods studied, large-scale conservation has been undertaken only in the Srodmiescie district of Cracow. In the others, the proportion of houses in a state of ruin ranged from 1.7 percent in Tarnow to 22.2 percent in Rzeszow. However, the general under-investment in social infrastructure, especially on new housing estates, means that some old central city neighbourhoods have retained significant retailing and service functions, and this enhances their residential attraction despite the very poor housing.

Table 7.3 shows the extent to which housing conditions in the study areas are worse than in their respective cities as a whole. The old neighbourhoods tend to be best off with respect to piped water, the main deficiencies being lack of bathrooms, hot water, flush toilets and the need to use coal for heating which contributes to pollution. In terms of basic utilities, the quality of housing in these neighbourhoods is better where there is a larger proportion of private multi-family structures and owners make the effort to raise the standard of their own flats. Housing units in the old neighbourhoods tend to be much older than in the city at large: the proportion built before 1918 ranges from 65 percent to 100 percent (except in Krosno where it is 35 percent, reflected in a higher standard of amenities) compared with 8 percent to 20 percent in the entire cities.

Small apartments, of one or two rooms, tend to predominate in the old town neighbourhoods, as Table 7.4 shows. Only in the Srodmiescie district of Cracow are there many larger apartments (over 80 m^2); this is associated with a revitalisation programme under which service functions are replacing residence in some buildings, with the remaining accommodation upgraded and reoccupied as 'luxurious' apartments - not by their former residents but by people in high administrative or social positions.

The old city neighbourhoods tend to be occupied disproportionately by older people, living mainly on retirement pensions and disability pay. There are also relatively high proportions of females and single persons. Better apartments in new housing estates in the outer parts of the city have led to a move of high-status people out of the old inner neighbourhoods. This has often been hastened by an inflow of an 'undesirable element'. The effect has been a gradual process of reduction of the social status of the people residing in the old neighbourhoods.

Table 7.3   Basic amenities of housing units in old city neighbourhoods (OC) compared with the entire city (EC) 1978

City	% of housing units equipped with:									
	piped water		flush toilet		gas		bathroom		central heating	
	OC	EC	OC	EC	OC	EC	OC	EC	OC	EC
Jaroslaw	62	76	40	66	77	80	31	63	11	45
Krosno	88	80	73	73	99	97	69	71	43	41
Nowy Sacz	96	83	69	73	9	52	52	69	11	50
Rzeszow	94	92	65	87	45	82	55	86	8	77
Tarnow	93	90	62	82	89	83	42	78	4	62
Cracow:		92		87		86		59		11
Kazimierz	96		78		86		59		11	
Srodmiescie	92		77		82		64		20	

Source: Prawelska-Skrzypek (1988, p. 227, Table 2)

Table 7.4   Size of housing units in old city neighbourhoods (OC) compared with the entire city (EC) 1978

City	% of units by number of rooms						% of units by living area			
	one		two		five or more		< 30 m²		> 80 m²	
	OC	EC	OC	EC	OC	EC	OC	EC	OC	EC
Jaroslaw	17	9	49	27	4	11	20	13	8	12
Krosno	15	7	28	18	5	14	18	11	10	14
Nowy Sacz	15	7	26	17	1	10	22	13	7	13
Rzeszow	26	7	45	21	1	9	18	10	4	8
Tarnow	7	17	44	25	1	8	23	24	7	9
Cracow		12		26		6		15		7
Kazimierz	17		39		2		19		10	
Srodmiescie	25		34		5		17		21	

Source: Prawelska-Skrzypek (1988, p. 227, Table 1)

However, despite considerable changes in population and economic ties of residents, the current social and occupational structure of the old town neighbourhoods is similar to that of the pre-war period. Table 7.5 shows higher proportions of people employed as labourers in the old town than in the entire city in Jaroslaw, Nowy Sacz and Rzeszow, with the reverse in the others. All but Krosno and the Srodmiescie district of Cracow have lower proportions of people with higher education in the old than the entire city. Only Srodmiescie has a lower proportion of people without occupational training than in its city at large.

From the cities studied, two types of old neighbourhoods could be distinguished. First, there are those not greatly disrupted by the war and functioning as trade and service centres for the entire city. This is exemplified by the Srodmiescie district, and also by Cracow's Old Town. The built environment is in a relatively good condition, and such neighbourhoods are characterised by an elite social structure, as in the pre-war period. Secondly, there are neighbourhoods near the city centre but only partially fulfilling central service functions. They suffered severely during the war, and are today characterised by poor built environment and housing conditions, and by the low social status of their populations. The status of the residents of the old districts of Polish cities is not as low as in the poor neighbourhoods in the west. Nevertheless, 'in a centrally planned economy, particular physical and spatial structures in cities attract particular social groups' (Prawelska-Skrzypek, 1988, p. 231).

Table 7.5 **Selected characteristics of the social and occupational structure of the population of old city neighbourhoods (OC) compared with the entire city (EC) 1978**

City	% employed as labourers		% with higher education		% without occupational training	
	O C	E C	O C	E C	O C	E C
Jaroslaw	54	39	3	6	52	41
Krosno	42	43	9	8	42	39
Nowy Sacz	47	40	5	7	47	37
Rzeszow	48	35	6	12	44	31
Tarnow	45	46	4	8	50	39
Cracow:		44		13		33
Kazimierz	41		11		38	
Srodmiescie	28		21		27	

Source: Prawelska-Skrzypek (1988, p.229, Table 4)

Conclusion

This chapter had added further evidence to that provided by Warsaw, to demonstrate the spatial association between socio-occupational status of the population and attributes of their area of residence. That the outcome conflicts with socialist egalitarian ideology is clear. What is also evident from the recent Polish experience is that a people offered firm expectations of a better life under socialism, in terms both of material living standards and social justice, will not necessarily accept something different. Obviously, there will be those who welcome the opportunity to become unequal, occupying a single-family villa or luxury flat in some attractive inner-city neighbourhood or building a nice house beyond the city fringe. And there will also be those to whom the ordinary provision of the state is a welcome improvement on the old city slum or village hovel. But large numbers of working people are not satisfied, and have found a means of expressing dissent through Solidarity. The impact on Polish government and society is a matter of continuing interest, not least as an indication of the capacity of 'socialism' to change.

8. SUMMARY AND CONCLUSIONS

'cities in Eastern Europe are "socialist" not in the sense that they are necessarily better or worse than they used to be, or better or worse than comparable cities in capitalist countries. They are socialist in that they are *different*.'
I. Szelenyi (1983)

The preceding chapters should have made it clear that the cities which we have examined are significantly different from those more familiar to us from first-hand or text-book experience, at least with respect to our focus on inequality. This concluding chapter begins by briefly setting the socialist city in historical context, and then summarises the evidence as to the distinctive patterns of urban inequality manifest under East European socialism and the processes behind them. Finally, we offer some speculations about the future of the socialist city.

The socialist city in history

An interpretation of history sometimes associated with Marxism is that one form of society follows another in sequence, as a particular kind of socio-economic organisation generates conditions which frustrate its ongoing reproduction. Thus, in Europe, feudalism was replaced by capitalism under the pressure of new technologies which required more flexible use of labour than was possible under the old order dominated by large landowners in the countryside and craft guilds in the cities. Similarly, capitalism is expected to be replaced by socialism, as a working class - increasingly impoverished by exploitation on the part of competing employers - seek liberation through revolution. The ultimate emergence of 'true' communism completes the transition.

Each kind of society has its own distinctive spatial form, including that of its cities. Just as inadequacies of general social structure contribute to change, so does the prevailing spatial form of society. For example, the congested medieval city constrained by its walls required reconstruction or replacement by new towns if industry was to expand. The squalor and gross social disparities of the Victorian capitalist city stimulated slum clearance and other civic initiatives to improve the lives of the poor and preserve social order. As spatial form changes, so does social structure, in a continuing process of interaction one with another. It is in this sense that cities both reflect and are reflected in the broader society.

In working towards a theory of intra-urban structure of Polish cities, Weclawowicz (1981) attempts to set the socialist city in historical context. Table 8.1 shows the 'socio-economic formations' of feudalism, capitalism and socialism, their predominant socio-spatial patterns, and the processes shaping the city. The division of feudal society into a small elite and a much larger lower class created a strong spatial dichotomy, with the elite concentrated in the centre of the city and social status diminishing outwards along with districts differentiated by occupation as well as ethnicity and religion. This is essentially the 'preindustrial' city as identified by G. Sjoberg. To this horizontal segregation was added the vertical differentiation arising from people of varied social status living and working one above the other in multi-functional buildings (e.g. servants' quarters above master's residence above a shop). Under capitalism, spatial segregation according to class came to predominate, with political power and social status arising largely from income, and the urban land market driven by the overall profit imperative as the major forces involved. Under socialism, the broad socio-spatial segregation of the capitalist city is replaced by a mosaic pattern of occupational-status disparities, as housing policy reflects the social (state) evaluation of different kinds of labour, along with some egalitarian planning.

While this scheme was originally developed from research in one country, it can claim more general validity. Even though the countries which we have examined reveal their own distinctive features, they all appear different from those under capitalism (and feudalism) with respect both to patterns of intra-urban inequality and the processes responsible. We will consider these two facets in turn.

Table 8.1 Intra-urban patterns in cities of different socio-economic formations

Socio-economic formation	Predominant form of socio-spatial patterns in the city	Processes and forces shaping social pattern in the city
Feudalism	Horizontal segregation according to status, occupation, ethnicity and religion. Vertical segregation according to social position.	Production structure: level of technology and guilds system. Social status, custom.
Capitalism	Spatial (horizontal) segregation of social groups according to class, ethnic and religious origin, stage in life cycle (zonal, sectoral and multiple nuclei models).	Power structure. Social status. Land rent. The profit imperative.
Socialism	Decline of socio-spatial segregation. Emergence of mosaic patterns. Differentiation of occupational strata.	Social value of labour. Housing policy. Egalitarian planning.

Source: based on Weclawowicz (1981, p. 182, Table 1)

Patterns of inequality

Among both indigenous and western students of inequality in the East European and Soviet city there is almost universal agreement that the degree of social segregation and inequality under socialism is less than under capitalism. However, there are substantial differences in interpretation of both the spatial form or pattern of inequality and its extent, which are difficult to resolve. It is hard to judge competing claims, based on limited data, applying to varied times or periods, from different countries, and subjected to different forms of analysis. At the risk of simplification, two schools of thought may be identified.

The first argues that urban inequalities have been very greatly reduced under socialism, and that what does exist can best be described as a mosaic or patchwork, or in similar terms. This is essentially the conclusion arrived at by Weclawowicz in Poland. French and Hamilton (1979, pp. 16-17) reflect this view as follows:

> Everywhere, social segregation of the socialist city by *sectors* is absent or very greatly diminished, although in each city there is a tendency for some social segregation by apartment *building* to be found. In part, relative homogeneity of the occupational composition of the work force in industrial cities facilitates such uniformity. Nevertheless, in *any* city the low, largely nominal and relatively uniform rents for state-owned apartments means that no part of the city is barred to any inhabitant or migrant on the grounds of cost, income, status, or race.

They suggest that, in the larger polyfunctional cities with the entire range of occupations, segregation can occur by people occupying particular wedges convenient to their places of work, with different activities and hence types of employees concentrated in different parts of the city (e.g. in Moscow), but that this tendency is diminished substantially by the actual practice of longer-distance commuting on public transport at nominal flat-rate fares accompanied by social mixing in the micro-districts and housing blocks.

This view has been challenged by Dangschat (1987) in particular. He found 'surprisingly high' segregation of social groups by education, age and household size in Warsaw, contradicting what he describes as the conventional wisdom of a low rate of segregation in the socialist city. He is particularly critical of French and Hamilton and some Polish scholars. In place of the mosaic pattern or segregation at the level of the apartment block, this alternative view claims the existence of relatively large and socially homogeneous areas in socialist cities. In a review of earlier experience and recent research, Szelenyi (1987, p. 6) is sympathetic to Dangschat's analysis:

> due to public ownership of most central urban land, due to the uniquely state socialist, exceptionally high degree of concentration of financing and of construction-firms, [an] unusually high proportion of new urban housing in socialist cities is being built in large estates, in a geographically concentrated way. Socialist city planning creates large geographic areas which are quite homogeneous in terms of the nature and quality of their housing stock and, as follows logically [from privileged, class-specific access to housing], they are also homogeneous in terms of the occupational composition of their inhabitants.

Thus Szelenyi still sees the differentiation of urban space very much as revealed in his earlier research on Hungarian cities.

There is some evidence in the cases presented in this publication to support both points of view. However, they seem as much if not more the outcome of the particular method used, and especially of the level of spatial disaggregation adopted, as of the reality they attempt to portray. In Moscow, the city where firm numerical data are hardest to find, there is some indication of broad zones of differentiation (inequality) at the level of the 30 or so districts/boroughs, yet a finer level of subdivision reveals patterns which could fairly be described as mosaics. Similarly in Warsaw, Dangschat's broad zones yield to something considerably more complex at the scale adopted by Weclawowicz here and in some other Polish cities, and by Jagielski in Wroclaw.

The most plausible resolution of these alternative views would appear to be that some broad spatial differentiation or inequality in occupational status, education, housing, certain demographic characteristics, and (less conspicuously) income is very likely to be found in medium-sized and large cities, but punctuated by smaller distinctive areas differentiated by the survival of pre-war/pre-Revolutionary housing, enclaves of superior or inferior state housing or co-operatives. Much will depend on the history of the city in question, its pattern of (re)development, and the survival or otherwise of distinctive social areas, local communities or environments. The existence of ethnic areas will depend on how far ethnicity has persisted as a means of group identity in the face of the new ideology, as well as on surviving or otherwise the 'holocaust' or planned resettlement.

Attempts to use familiar western descriptive models as means of generalisation have not proved particularly helpful, as we have seen. It may be possible to detect elements of concentric zones or wedges in the spatial pattern of socio-economic differentiation in many cities, but their significance is diminished by the absence of the economic rationale arising from the operation of the urban land market, which enables these models to make some sense of the capitalist city.

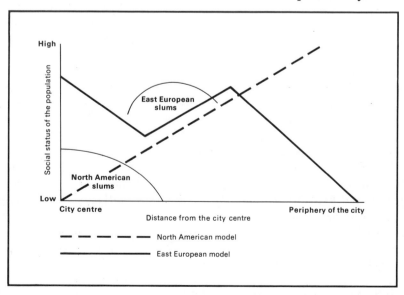

Figure 8.1 Social status and distance from the city centre in East European and American cities
Source: based on Szelenyi (1983, p. 148, Fig. 7.2)

However, Szelenyi (1983, pp. 147-8) has proposed a simple generalisation which relates social status to distance from the city centre. Figure 8.1 shows high status associated with a central location - the reverse of what would be expected for the most part, in the city in North America and the rest of the advanced capitalist world. Social status then falls away with distance , to reach what Szelenyi refers to as the slums of the transitional zone, where deteriorating property still awaits redevelopment. Status rises again in the multi-storey estates, with the best new housing and best urban services - albeit perhaps delayed in their provision. The outer suburbs of private homes, usually with very poor services, are for the working class, and are the lowest status areas in the city even if the inhabitants may be satisfied with their housing conditions. The extent to which such a concentric zone pattern will be interrupted by wedges and more local variation will depend on conditions specific to individual cities, and also to the mosaic tendency which appears to be a stronger characteristic of the East European city under socialism than Szelenyi recognises.

The process of inequality

Let us now turn to the process whereby socio-economic differentiation or inequality arises in the socialist city. While this will be different from what occurs under capitalism, residential segregation can be expected in any society if certain conditions are met. Following Dangschat (1987), these are: socio-economic disparities within urban society, variable housing stock, spatial concentrations of differing housing conditions, and competition for dwellings within the housing system. To these might be added differences in local levels of service provision and general environmental quality, which may be closely associated with differences in housing but can act independently. And some residential sorting can also be expected to arise from the existence of distinctive ethnic or cultural groups, as well as from variations in family structure which lead to residential selectivity. All these conditions are in fact met, to a greater or lesser extent, in the countries which we have examined, and it is worth considering how they come about under socialism as contributors to the process of inequality.

Socio-economic disparities arise to a large exetent from the division of labour. In any modern industrial society people's roles are differentiated: some work primarily with their hands, others with their minds, and within this broad dichotomy there will be many and varied occupations. Under capitalism the occupational structure is strongly reflected in income differentials, which are themselves the key to other sources of inequality in material consumption and services. Under socialism the social (i.e. state) evaluation of different occupations is less clearly defined in attributes that sharply differentiate people's living standards. And there may be a deliberate attempt to assign high status to manual labour and lower status than in the west to professional occupations. Nevertheless, there are unequal rewards, as part of an incentive system designed to attract people into crucial roles - whether elite leadership positions or miners in some inhospitable location. Social stratification therefore does exist under socialism, though less pronounced and with some different characteristics when compared with capitalism.

Dissimilarities in housing stock arise in various ways. They are an inevitable outcome of the historical development of the socialist city, or part of the city, as standards of design, construction and fittings change - usually for the better but sometimes for the worse. There may have been a high quality of state provision in the first phase of socialist construction, followed by deteriorating standards associated with mass provision as in the Khrushchev blocks in the USSR, followed again by improved quality. Special state accommodation may have been built for certain privileged or elite groups. The co-operative is a further source of differentiation, though its scale, quality and quasi-private status differs from one country to another. There is also the pre-socialist housing stock, varying from the occasional palace and the detached villas of the bourgeoisie to the slum tenements of the old industrial quarters such as Warsaw's Praga. Finally there is the private or market-sector stock of the socialist period itself, usually of poor standard by conventional criteria compared with state provision but including some fine homes in some countries where high incomes can be earned and spent on private housing.

The association of level of service provision with housing quality is close but not complete. Overall, the inner city has the largest concentration of specialised services and the best access to the city-wide service network. But some well-serviced inner areas may have poor housing and environment, as we observed in Poland. The new estates may have good-quality housing, but suffer from time-lags in service provision as well as being remote from central facilities. Some inequality is intrinsic to a spatial hierarchy of service provision, as we saw in Moscow.

That disparities in housing and associated local environmental conditions have a spatial expression in the socialist city is clear. This follows from the outward growth of the city, and from the planning practice of creating fairly large and homogeneous estates. It is also an outcome of the pre-socialist inheritance. The superficial uniformity of the newer housing estates which tend to dominate the modern socialist city can create a misleading impression of the extent to which the form of the city has changed. It may in fact still be very much a reflection of its past. This is not only because housing has survived from an earlier era but also because in other respects the pre-socialist form may have been preserved. For example, Regulska (1987, pp. 327, 333) points out that in the initial post-war phase of reconstruction, limitations on resources directed urban policy towards those areas which required least investment, thus reproducing the pre-war urban network; old housing was also preserved to reduce the requirement for building new apartments. The immediate need to repair any factory which could be used, as in Warsaw after the war, meant that little attention could be given to such matters as land use zoning (French and Hamilton, 1979, p. 371). So in these and other ways, elements of the spatial form and differentiation of the pre-socialist city have contributed to the opportunities for inequality today.

Competition for housing and environment of differing quality arises from shortage, not only of housing in general but also of the kind people prefer. Some individuals are better placed than others to succeed in this competition. This may be a matter of need, such as existing housing conditions or family size, qualifying people for state provision. But it can also reflect privileged access on the part of those in certain occupations. In the period immediately following the advent of socialism there was a strong ideological and practical commitment to rehousing the poor working class, demonstrated in the appropriation and redistribution of large houses of the bourgeoisie. With the passage of time priorities appear to have changed. There is evidence in the cases presented in earlier chapters of better educated people in conventionally 'higher' occupational groups or of elite status being advantaged in access to housing. Even in the USSR, where state control of residential space seems tighter than elsewhere in Eastern Europe, those who are able can 'work the system'; for example, there in anecdotal evidence of the wife of a scientific worker spending most of her time trying to find a better flat - they moved nine times before settling on a nice place in a good older block in central Moscow. They had the time and knowledge; others do not.

In all the countries considered here, there is ample evidence of differentiation of residential space on objective grounds of housing quality and service provision. There is also evidence that people are aware of differences. They may not appraise the urban environment in the same way that objective indicators might suggest, as we found in Warsaw, but they perceive a differentiated residential space according to their own values and needs. And within the limits of their personal ability, the rigidities of the state housing allocation system, and what may exist of a market sector, they make choices and do their best to implement them.

In the usual interpretation of the capitalist city, spatial residential sorting arises from personal mobility, as people take their variable incomes into a spatially differentiated housing market or remain where they are because they are satisfied or cannot afford to move. Spatial sorting under socialism is of a different kind. Much is directed, or at least facilitated, by the state or city authorities. Those like the Muscovites who exercise western-style freedom of choice are very much a minority, the size of which will vary with the country concerned. Dangschat (1987, pp. 56-7) makes the point that low mobility contributes to residential segregation, as in Warsaw where the general housing shortage leads to those selected for a new housing estate on similar criteria staying there. This helps to explain the fact that similarity of family size and stage in life cycle may be as much if not more of a feature of residential segregation in the socialist city than western-style economic status.

Once residential segregation has been established, the inequalities may be self-reinforcing. Szelenyi (1983, p. 105) sees the process as follows:

If districts have different housing classes and social strata, they generate different needs under

72

non-market conditions as well as under market conditions. They also generate different capacities to get what they want, by fighting or bargaining or any other means. People in middle-class districts have more contacts, they have more of the skills required in bureaucratic negotiations, they have better access to many sources of information. So a segregated middle-class district will often attract a department store before a working-class district does, and it will often get a larger share of the urban services and infrastructure that its residents want. Those advantages will be superimposed on the housing advantages such districts already possess. Meanwhile segregated working-class districts will suffer the corresponding disadvantages; their life-style and opportunities of mobility will suffer accordingly; so will their individual and collective capacities to do anything effective about the inequalities from which they suffer. In such districts the physical deterioration of the housing runs parallel to changes in the composition of the residents, leaving generally lower incomes, and declining standards in important local services and institutions, especially the schools.

If this process seems reminiscent of that in the capitalist city, it is important to recognise that what led to the initial pattern of segregation is significantly different, as is the way in which additional local advantages may be secured. There is a temptation to see parallels with capitalism, and indeed to assert that Eastern European socialism is not really very different. However, the vast majority of those who study the socialist city find a distinctive process of inequality at work. Even Dangschat (1987, p. 56), who sees close similarities in the pattern of inequality in Warsaw and the capitalist city, recognises that, 'residential segregation processes in Warsaw are different from those in west European cities'. And Szelenyi, the first Eastern European scholar to give detailed attention to inequalities in the socialist city, continues to assert that they are different from those under capitalism, as the quotation which begins this chapter indicates. He elaborates as follows (Szelenyi, 1987, pp. 4-5):

the state socialist society is producing and reproducing social inequalities, because its economic system is structured in a certain way, because it is built on redistributive mechanisms, upon which the distribution of power and privilege is based in these societies. If one wants to alter in a significant way these inequalities one will have to modify the underlying economic structure.

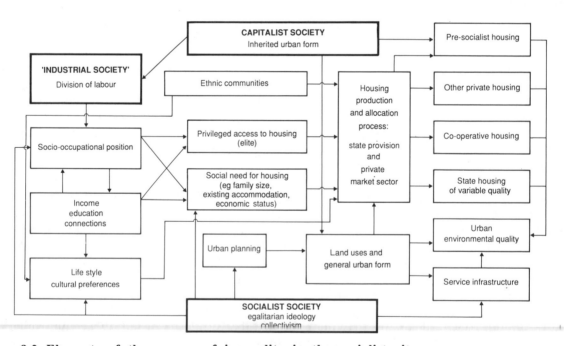

Figure 8.2 Elements of the process of inequality in the socialist city.

The broad features of this structure are sketched out in Figure 8.2, along with other elements contributing to inequality. On the right of the diagram is the differentiated housing stock, service infrastructure and local environmental quality, patterned by pre-socialist forms as well as by new urban development. To the left is a suggestion of the process whereby differential access arises, from the production and redistributive mechanisms and the role of individuals within them. While details may require modification in the light of how particular societies function nationally, this is general enough to capture the essence of East European socialism as an inegalitarian system.

The future of the socialist city

What we have observed and tried to comprehend, then, is what was described at the outset as the central paradox of socialist society: the continuing existence of inequality in a society built on egalitarian ideals. To quote Szelenyi (1987, p. 7) again, 'An ideologically egalitarian housing policy and urban planning produced an inegalitarian system of housing allocation, and produced, and keeps reproducing, the residential segregation of occupational groups'. It is not that those who run the societies concerned somehow deliberately subvert the system: 'They create inegalitarian cities not because they wish to do so, but because they operate as key agents in a new social structure, which is shaped by new types of class antagonisms'. We will conclude with some speculations on what scope there might be for change in such a structure.

The idea that societies reproduce themselves, including their patterns of inequality, is central to understanding social development or change. It was introduced at the start of the chapter, in the discussion of the progression from feudalism to capitalism and on to socialism: societies tend to reproduce their essential form, until some basic functional failure induces change which may be revolutionary but more often takes the form of evolution (see Smith, 1988, pp. 33-7 for further discussion). What is the significance of our observation and understanding of inequality under socialism for the process of change ?

One possible interpretation is that the emerging and self-reproducing patterns of inequality will greatly constrain change in the direction of a truly egalitarian society. Privilege and its spatial expression may become entrenched, so that those in advantaged positions will preserve the status quo and prevent completion of the supposed transition from socialism to full communism. That this might be the case in the USSR was suggested in an earlier discussion of inequality in the Soviet city (Smith, 1979, pp. 360-2). French (1987, pp. 316-17) sees 'an element of convergence between the Soviet and the Western city - greater social segregation and the identification of prestige areas, the increasing importance of the car, patterns of shopping activity and commuting', in what he describes as a new stage in Soviet urban development. Andrusz (1984, pp. 279-80) envisages a form of suburbanisation on the part of higher-status groups, moving out of the city and commuting western-style but keeping a flat in the city centre. At the heart of what is taking place is a growing materialism, as Soviet and other socialist citizens seek to ape their western counterparts, accompanied by an individualism and privatisation of everyday life which is in sharp contradiction to the collective identity that is supposed to shape the new socialist man/woman. Andrusz (1987, pp. 491-2) sees the significance of current developments for the city as follows:

> the present trend suggests that the working out of the contradiction between individualistic tendencies inherent in the growing home-centredness on the one hand and collectivist ideals embodied in the widespread use of public services on the other in likely to intensify. This raises the issue of the type of architecture and built environment which best corresponds to the set of norms and values which may be imputed to the more privatized, consumer-oriented, home-centred, car-ownership-seeking nuclear family with segmented role playing that is emerging in the Soviet Union.

Andrusz considers that the present period of reconstruction (*perestroika*) associated with the Gorbachev reforms is likely to be reflected in urban forms which express equality in the public realm but make more allowance for individual differences in needs and perceptions in private life. This could make for more variety in apartment design and layout. If the release of individual creativity and initiative is central to the reforms, this could result in more scope for personal expression in the urban environment. And economic reforms which encourage an element of co-operative (quasi-private) business could increase income differentials and generate more material socio-economic inequality with a spatial expression, while political reforms could erode elite privilege. But while elements in the existing society are stimulating change, so the inherited built form will constrain it, just as it has the creation of the socialist city on its capitalist past. The huge, uniform housing estates will remain for a long time to come and will not readily yield to new forces of differentiation.

In some respects the Soviet Union may be pointing the way towards a new East European socialism, but its form and the extent to which it really constitutes a radical departure from the past is still not clear. In some respects the Soviet Union may merely be moving towards the greater flexibility which characterises residential sorting in most other East European countries. But that all is not necessarily well in such countries as Poland and Czechoslovakia is a matter of current, almost daily news. The USSR has avoided a mass movement of the working class of the kind seen in Poland and, more spasmodically, in some other countries. Perhaps it will change in time, in response to clearly detected if less overtly articulated discontent. That the disaffection of the masses has at least some of its origin in the inequality of urban life is evident from the Polish experience. Whether the outcome here and elsewhere will be more equal cities is an open question; they may simply come more closely to resemble those of not particularly affluent capitalist countries. But whatever the future of the socialist city, its past as well as the distinctive nature of its own changing society will ensure that it remains different, and a continuing source of geographical curiosity.

К ЗИМНЕМУ СЕЗОНУ...

Рисунок М. БИТНОГО

Epilogue

'For the winter season': *cartoon comment on consumerism in the Soviet Union, with its portent of increasing individualism and material inequality in socialist urban society (from the Soviet satirical magazine Krokodil).*

BIBLIOGRAPHY AND SOURCES

Andrusz, G.D. (1984) **Housing and Urban Development in the USSR**, Macmillan, London

Andrusz, G.D. (1987) The built environment in Soviet theory and practice, **International Journal of Urban and Regional Research**, 11, pp. 478-98

Arkady (1981) **Warsaw: Portrait of a City**, Arkady, Warsaw

Barbash, N.B. (1982) Spatial relations among places with complementary functions within the city of Moscow, **Soviet Geography**, 23, pp. 77-94

Barbash, N.B. (1983) Physical development of infants as an indicator of the condition of the urban environment, **Soviet Geography**, 24, pp. 204-13

Barbash, N.B. and Gutnov A.E. (1980) Urban planning aspects of the spatial organization of Moscow, **Soviet Geography**, 11, pp. 557-73

Bartnicki, S.P. (1986) The geography of crime: a case study of Warsaw, **Miscellanea Geographica**, Warsaw, pp. 237-42

Bater, J.H. (1980) **The Soviet City: Ideal and Reality**, Edward Arnold, London

Bater, J.H. (1984) The Soviet city: continuity and change in privilege and place, in J.A. Agnew, J. Mercer and D.E. Sopher (eds) **The City in Cultural Context**, Allen and Unwin, Boston, pp. 134-62

Bater, J.H. (1986) Some recent perspectives on the Soviet city, **Urban Geography**, 7, 93-102

Bond (1988) Moscow under restructuring: Introduction to the Special Issue **Soviet Geography**, 14, pp. 1-15.

Ciechocinska, M. (1987) Government intervention to balance housing supply and urban population growth: the case of Warsaw, **International Journal of Urban and Regional Research**, 11, pp. 9-26

Dangschat, J. (1987) Sociospatial disparities in a 'socialist' city: the case of Warsaw at the end of the 1970s, **International Journal of Urban and Regional Research**, 11, pp. 37-60

Dangschat, J. and Blasius, J. (1987) Social and spatial disparities in Warsaw in 1978: an application of correspondence analysis to a 'socialist' city, **Urban Studies**, 24, pp. 173-91

Danta, D.R. (1987) Hungarian urbanization and socialist ideology, **Urban Geography**, 8, pp. 391-404

Demko, G.J. and Regulska, J. (1987) Socialism and its impact on urban processes and the city, **Urban Geography**, 8, pp. 289-92

French, R.A. (1987) Changing spatial patterns in Soviet cities - planning or pragmatism? **Urban Geography**, 8, pp. 309-20

French, R.A. and Hamilton, F.E.I. (eds) (1979) **The Socialist City: Spatial Structure and Urban Policy**, John Wiley, Chichester

Friedrichs, J. (1988) Large cities in Eastern Europe, in M. Dogan and J.K. Kasarda (eds) **The Metropolis Era: Vol. 1 A World of Giant Cities**, Sage, Beverley Hills, pp. 128-54

Gomostayeva, G.A. (1986) Social infrastructure levels in the largest cities of the USSR: a measure of the quality of life, **Soviet Geography**, 27, pp. 368-76

Grime, K. and Weclawowicz, G. (1981) Warsaw, in M. Pacione (ed.) **Urban Problems and Planning in the Developed World**, Croom Helm, London, pp. 258-91

Hall, P. (1984) **The World Cities**, Weidenfeld and Nicolson, London, pp. 116-39

Hamilton, F.E.I. (1976) **The Moscow City Region**, Oxford University Press, Oxford

Hamilton, F.E.I. (1978) The East European and Soviet city, **Geographical Magazine**, May, pp. 511-15

Hegedus, J. (1987) Reconsidering the roles of the state and the market in socialist housing systems, **International Journal of Urban and Regional Research**, 11, pp. 79-97

Hegedus, J. (1988) Inequalities in East European cities: a reply to Ivan Szelenyi, **International Journal of Urban and Regional Research**, 12, pp. 129-32

Hegedus, J. and Tosics, I. (1983) Housing classes and housing policy: some changes in the Budapest housing market. **International Journal of Urban and Regional Research**, 7, pp. 467-94

Jagielski, A. (1986) La dimension socio-demographique de l'espace urbain polonais, **Espace Populations Sociétés**, pp. 145-52

Malicka, W. (1979) Housing estates and town communities in postwar Poland, **International Journal of Urban and Regional Research**, 3, pp. 209-19

Mateju, P., Vecernik, J. and Jerabek, H. (1979) Social structure, spatial structure and problems of urban research: the example of Prague, **International Journal of Urban and Regional Research**, 3, pp. 181-200

Morton, H.W. and Stuart, R.C. (eds) (1984) **The Contemporary Soviet City**, Macmillan, London

Musil, J. (1968) The development of Prague's ecological structure, in R.E. Pahl (ed.) **Readings in Urban Sociology**, Pergamon Press, Oxford, pp. 232-59

Musil, J. (1987) Housing policy and the sociospatial structure of cities in a socialist country: the example of Prague, **International Journal of Urban and Regional Research**, 11, pp. 27-37

Musil, J. and Rysavy, Z. (1983) Urban and regional processes under capitalism and socialism: a case study from Czechoslovakia, **International Journal of Urban and Regional Research**, 7, pp. 495-527

Nowakowski, S. (1979) Some aspects of postwar urban sociology, **International Journal of Urban and Regional Research**, 3, pp. 203-8

Portisch, H. (1972) **I Saw Siberia**, Harrap, London

Pounds, N.J.G., Dziewonski, K., Kortus, B. and Vlassenbroeck, W. (1981) The growth of Cracow and Nowa Huta, in A. Cochrane, C.Hamnett and L. McDowell (eds) **City, Economy and Society: A Comparative Reader**, Harper and Row, London, pp. 16-25

Prawelska-Skrzypek, G. (1988) Social differentiation in old central city neighbourhoods in Poland, **Area**, 20, pp. 221-32

Regulska, J. (1987) Urban development under socialism: the Polish experience, **Urban Geography**, 8, pp. 321-39

Rugg, D.S. (1972) **Spatial Foundations of Urbanism**, Wm. C. Brown, Dubuque, Iowa, pp. 244-65

Rukavishnikov, V.O. (1978) Ethnosocial aspects of population distribution in cities of Tataria, **Soviet Sociology**, 8, pp. 59-79

Shaw, D.J.B. (1983) The Soviet urban general plan and recent advances in Soviet urban planning, **Urban Studies**, 20, pp. 393-403

Sieminski, W. (1979) The social goals of residential communities in Poland, **International Journal of Urban and Regional Research**, 3, pp. 220-7

Sillince, J.A.A. (1985a) Housing as social problem versus housing as historical problem: the case of Hungary, **Environment and Planning C**, 3, pp. 299-318

Sillince, J.A.A. (1985b) The housing market of the Budapest urban region 1949-1983, **Urban Studies**, 22, pp. 141-9

Smith, D.M. (1978) Siberian city of science, **Geographical Magazine**, 63, pp. 238-42

Smith, D.M. (1979) **Where the Grass is Greener: Living in an Unequal World**, Penguin, Harmondsworth

Smith, D.M. (1988) **Geography, Inequality and Society**, Cambridge Univesity Press, Cambridge

Swianiewicz, P. (1986) Varied attractiveness of urban terrains: the case of Warsaw, **Miscellanea Geographica**, Warsaw, pp. 223-35

Szelenyi, I. (1983) **Urban Inequalities under State Socialism**, Oxford Universtity Press, Oxford

Szelenyi, I. (1987) Housing inequalities and occupational segregation in state socialist cities: commentary on the special issue of IJURR on east European cities, **International Journal of Urban and Regional Research**, 11, pp. 1-8

Thomas, C. (1988) Moscow's mobile millions, **Geography**, 73, pp. 216-25

Tosics, I. (1987) Privatization in housing policy: the case of the western countries and that of Hungary, **International Journal of Urban and Regional Research**, 11, pp. 61-78

Tosics, I. (1988) Inequalities in East European cities: can redistribution ever be equalizing, and if so, why should we avoid it? A reply to Ivan Szelenyi, **International Journal of Urban and Regional Research**, 12, pp. 133-6

Vasil'yev G.L. and Privalova, O.L. (1984) A social-geographic evaluation of differences within a city, **Soviet Geography**, 25, pp. 488-96

Weclawowicz, G. (1975) **The structure of socio-economic space of Warsaw 1931 and 1970 in the light of factor analysis**, Polish Academy of Sciences, Warsaw

Weclawowicz, G. (1981) Towards a theory of intra-urban structures of Polish cities, Geographia Polonica, 44, pp. 179-200

Weclawowicz, G. (1985) The socio-spatial structure of Radom city in 1978, **Geographia Polonica**, 51, pp. 85-98

Yanitsky, O. (1986) Urbanization in the USSR: theory, tendencies and policy, **International Journal of Urban and Regional Research**, 10, pp. 265-87

Zovanyi, G. (1986) Structural changes in a system of urban places: the 20th century evolution of Hungary's urban settlement network, **Regional Studies**, 20, pp. 47-71